BRENDA COSTIGAN

For Goodness Sake

COOKBOOK

© Brenda Costigan 1992

Printed November 1992

ISBN 0-9514115-1-9

Photography - Neil Macdougald

Cooking and Food Styling - Brenda Costigan and Catherine McDonald.

Acknowledgement to Goodalls (CPC Foods) for use of some of the photographs.

Grateful thanks to Aston Colour Press Limited for their patience and advice.

All rights reserved. No part of this publication may be reproduced, stored in a retrieval system or transmitted in any form or by any means, electronic, mechanical, photocopying, recording or otherwise without prior permission of Crescent Press (Publisher).

My sincere thanks to Mary Burke for her typing and editing skills. Special thanks to Ann Macdougald for her floral and styling skills. Thanks also to the O'Donnell family for their encouragement and to my children Catherine, Peter and David for their invaluable help.

For Dick - who made it all possible - with love.

Published by Crescent Press (Publishers)
3 Sycamore Crescent
Mount Merrion
Co. Dublin, Ireland.

A catalogue record for this book is available from the British Library

Contents

Introduction

This is my second cookery book! It is a collection of some more of my favourite recipes selected with healthy eating in mind. The recipes I include are easy to cook and use readily available ingredients. All are family and friend tested!

Like a constant drip of water that wears a hole in a stone, the food we eat everyday has far more of an effect on us than the occasional splurge or indeed the occasional diet. Nutrition is an intricate matter but I have a thumbnail guide to good eating which keeps me on the straight and narrow - most of the time!

Since no one single food can supply all the nutrients we need - the most important rule for healthy eating is to EAT A WIDE VARIETY OF FOODS - IN MODERATION!

Ideally CHOOSE FOODS AS NEAR TO THEIR NATURAL STATE AS POSSIBLE. For example, a fresh eating apple is nutritionally better than a carton of apple juice - or a steamed potato in it's jacket is better than a packet of instant mash.

GO EASY ON FAT, GO EASY ON SALT, I swear by freshly ground black pepper, it has such good flavour, it compensates for reduced salt. GO EASY ON SUGAR!

However food is to be enjoyed, it is one of life's pleasures. Hopefully you will get pleasure and enjoyment trying out my recipes. I also include my wedding cake recipe, which is in constant demand.

Good Cooking !

Brenda Costigan

Soups, Snacks and Light Meals

(Q) = quick to cook   (F) = suitable for freezing

These recipes are a collection of ideas suitable to serve as starters or light meals. Soups can fall into either of these categories. Indeed, soups are one of the great basics of cookery. I love those meal-in-a-bowl type soups like my Vegetable and Bacon Soup. This is a great family favourite. For speed and flavour, the Spaghetti Carbonara and the Quick Vienna Pizza are terrific, whilst the Spanish Omelette makes a meal from little bits and pieces.

One of the golden rules of healthy eating is to eat a variety of different foods. Soups are an excellent way of including a number of different ingredients.

Vegetable and Bacon Soup

(Serves 6)

A real favourite of mine! It is a real 'meal-in-a-bowl' soup. Especially handy when everyone seems to be eating at different times (like Saturdays) - individual servings can be reheated quickly in a little saucepan or in the microwave.

4-6 rashers (see note)
40 g (1½ oz) margarine or oil
1 large onion, chopped
2 cloves garlic, crushed or chopped
2 sticks celery, chopped
1 large carrot, diced
2 large potatoes, diced
1.1 litres (2 pts) water
1 tin chopped tomatoes
1 chicken stock cube
1 level teaspoon herbes de Provence (or mixed herbs)
1 bay leaf (optional)
Salt and freshly ground black pepper

To serve — 2-3 tablespoons chopped fresh parsley

Note: The rashers give great flavour to this soup. Use back or streaky as you prefer. Often I use cooked ham or bacon (225 g/8 oz), diced, instead OR a vacuum packet of bacon steaks (diced).

Chop the rashers and fry in the margarine in a large saucepan until golden. (If using cooked bacon, ham or bacon steaks, these need not be fried, simply add to the soup with the tinned tomatoes.)

Add the onion and fry with the rashers for a minute or two, then add in the garlic. Now you add in all the remaining ingredients. Bring to the boil. Cover with a lid and simmer gently until the vegetables are tender (about 30 minutes). Remove the bay leaf. Stir the parsley through the soup.

It is not necesary to thicken this soup but you can if you like. Simply blend 4 rounded teaspoons of cornflour with a little water to make a paste. Add to the soup when vegetables are tender. Bring to the boil, stirring briskly to thicken.

Variation with milk: Omit the tin of chopped tomatoes, then when vegetables are tender, add 275 ml (½ pt) of milk blended with 3 rounded teaspoons of cornflour. Bring to the boil, stirring to thicken.

2

Vegetable and Smoked Fish Soup

Use the recipe for the Vegetable and Bacon Soup. Use only three of the rashers. Also use **225 g (8 oz) smoked fish** (cod or haddock). Dip fish in boiling water for 5 minutes. Remove the skin, and cut fish in chunks. Add to soup 15 minutes before vegetables are tender. Especially nice in the variation with milk.

Fruit and vegetables with strong colours — tomatoes, peppers, courgettes, carrots, apricots etc., are all rich in Vitamin A.

Minestrone

(Serves 6-8)

This Italian classic is a meal in a bowl. The colourful collection of vegetables seems inspired by the Mediterranean sunshine. In actual fact, it is quite quick to prepare. It is a really special soup.

3-4 lean rashers or 110 g (4 oz) cooked ham
2-3 tablespoons oil (olive or vegetable)
1-2 large onion(s)
2-4 cloves garlic
2 carrots, finely chopped
2 sticks celery, sliced thinly
1 large potato, diced
75-110 g (3-4 oz) macaroni (uncooked) (optional)
1.1 litres (2 pts) beef stock (see note)
1 tin chopped tomatoes
Salt and freshly ground black pepper
1 level teaspoon oregano (or herbes de Provence)
1 teaspoon sugar
½-1 tin red kidney beans (400 g/14 oz), drained
110 g (4 oz) frozen peas
110 g (4 oz) frozen sweetcorn
1 mugful of very finely shredded cabbage

To serve — Parmesan cheese

Note: Beef stock is the traditional stock for this soup; but I often use chicken stock. If neither is available, I use 2 beef stock cubes.

Fry the chopped rashers in the oil in a large saucepan. Then add in the onion and soften without browning. Add the garlic and fry.

Next add the chopped carrots (these take the longest to cook, so the smaller they are, the quicker they'll cook). Add in the celery, potato and macaroni. Then pour in the beef stock and tomatoes. Season with salt and pepper. Flavour with oregano and sugar.

Bring to the boil, and then simmer, with the lid on, for about 10 minutes to soften the vegetables somewhat. Now add the drained kidney beans, the frozen peas and corn (no need to thaw them) and the cabbage.

Bring the soup back to the boil again and simmer for about 10 minutes more until the vegetables are nicely tender.

Serve with Parmesan cheese.

Chinese Chicken (or Turkey) Soup (Q)

(Serves 5-6)

For something a little different, try this recipe. In true Chinese style, it requires the minimum amount of cooking and contains an intriguing collection of ingredients.

2 tablespoons oil
1 chicken breast, cut in small strips (see note)
50 g (2 oz) cashew nuts or flaked almonds
1 medium onion, very thinly sliced
1 level tablespoon cornflour
1.1 litres (2 pts) chicken or turkey stock (or 2 chicken stock cubes)
1 tablespoon soy sauce
1-2 carrots, cut into matchstick pieces (175 g/6 oz)
2 whole cloves
110 g (4 oz) fresh bean sprouts (or use from a jar, rinse off brine)
110 g (4 oz) cucumber, neatly diced
110 g (4 oz) small mushrooms, thinly sliced
Salt and freshly ground black pepper
1 teaspoon sugar

Heat the oil in a saucepan and lightly fry the chicken, cashew nuts and the onion for a few minutes without browning. Mix the cornflour with a little of the stock and then add it to the saucepan with the remainder of the stock. Add in the soy sauce and the carrots and bring to the boil stirring continuously. Cover with a lid and simmer for about 10 minutes until the carrots are tender. Now add in all the remaining ingredients and simmer for another 5 minutes until everything is very hot but the vegetables still have their 'bite'.

Serve very hot with crusty bread. (Remove the whole cloves).

Note: Leftover cooked turkey or cooked chicken can be used in this soup, don't add it at the start but wait until adding 'all the remaining ingredients'.

Creamy Chicken and Sweetcorn Soup (Q)

(Serves 5-6)

A tasty creamy soup made in a jiffy with some chopped roast chicken (bought in a shop!!) and some frozen sweetcorn.

2-3 tablespoons oil OR 40 g (1½ oz) margarine
1 onion, chopped
1-2 cloves garlic, crushed
50 g (2 oz) mushrooms, chopped
1 stick celery, chopped finely
25 g (1 oz) flour
570 ml (1 pt) water
1 chicken stock cube
570 ml (1 pt) milk
175 g (6 oz) chopped roast chicken
175 g (6 oz) sweetcorn
4-6 spring onions (scallions), cut thinly
2-3 pinches ground ginger
2-3 pinches allspice
2 tablespoons soy sauce

Fry the onion in the oil until soft. Add in the garlic, mushrooms and celery. Fry these together to soften somewhat (2-3 minutes). Stir in the flour, which makes everything a bit pasty. Pour in the water and add the stock cube. Use a wire whisk to stir very briskly, bringing slowly to the boil. Add in all the remaining ingredients and bring to the boil again. Then simmer for 5-10 minutes to mingle the flavours and serve.

Garlic Breaded Mushrooms

These make delicious 'finger food' for drinks parties or are suitable as a starter. Give flavour to the breadcrumbs to make these special.

2 tablespoons flour
Salt and freshly ground black pepper
450 g (1 lb) small fresh mushrooms washed and dried
150 g (5 oz) fresh breadcrumbs
1/2 small onion, very finely chopped
1-2 cloves garlic, crushed
½-1 level teaspoon herbes de Provence
(or mixed herbs)
1-2 eggs beaten

Dip:
6 tablespoons Mayonnaise
2 cloves garlic, crushed (approx.)

Put the flour into a plastic bag and add some salt and pepper. Toss the mushrooms in this, shaking off the excess. (This helps the beaten egg to stick to the mushrooms.)

Put the breadcrumbs into a bowl and mix in the onion, garlic and herbs, season with salt and pepper. Dip the floured mushrooms into the beaten egg (only do a few at a time) and then into the breadcrumbs. Gently press the crumb mixture onto each mushroom. Lay them side by side on a tray.

(You can do all of this preparation a few hours in advance. Then cook a few at a time in a deep fat fryer and fry until crispy and golden brown, Drain on paper towels.)

Dip: Mix the crushed garlic through the mayonnaise and put in a little bowl.

To serve as finger food: Place fried mushrooms on a large plate with cocktail sticks. Put a small bowl of the prepared mayonnaise on the plate also.

To serve as a starter: Put 4-6 mushrooms on individual little plates with a blob of the prepared mayonnaise. Decorate with a little salad.

Quick Vienna Roll Pizza (Q)

(Serves 4)

A lovely fat Vienna roll makes a tasty base for a pizza that can be prepared in seconds. If a wholegrain Vienna roll is available - all the better.

1 Vienna Roll

Tomato mixture:
1 small clove garlic, crushed
½ small onion, finely chopped
Tin chopped tomatoes (see note)
Salt and freshly ground black pepper
1 teaspoon sugar
Pinch nutmeg
½ teaspoon oregano

For top:
110-175 g (4-6 oz) grated cheese
(cheddar or mozzarella, or both)

Extras:
Chopped ham or pepperoni (110 g/4 oz)
Chopped pineapple, 2-3 tablespoons
Sweetcorn, 2-3 tablespoons

Note: Also suitable instead of the tin of chopped tomatoes is tomato pulp, available in jars. Usually this needs no extra flavouring.

Slit the Vienna roll in two and toast the cut sides under the grill. Meanwhile mix the garlic and onion into the chopped tomatoes and season with salt, pepper, sugar, nutmeg and the oregano. Spoon this tasty mixture over the toasted bread. Put on any 'extras' that you wish to include and then sprinkle the cheese all over the top.

Grill until cheese melts and browns lightly.

Spaghetti Carbonara (Q)

(Serves 4-6)

When you come in the door exhausted and starving, with nothing ready to eat, this is the recipe for you. Ten minutes flat and you can have a hearty meal on the table! (Carbon means ham.)

350-450 g (¾-1 lb) spaghetti
1 chicken stock cube
25 g (1 oz) margarine OR oil
4 lean rashers, chopped
½ small onion, chopped
1-2 cloves garlic, crushed or chopped
8 mushrooms, chopped
2-3 tomatoes, chopped
4 eggs, lightly whisked
4 tablespoons milk (or cream!)
Salt and freshly ground black pepper
1 tablespoon butter or margarine
1-2 tablespoons chopped fresh parsley

To serve:
Grated Parmesan cheese (optional)

Cook the spaghetti in plenty of boiling water to which the chicken stock cube has been added.

While it cooks, fry the rashers in the margarine in a pan until golden. Lift them out and drain on kitchen paper. Then fry the onion, garlic and mushrooms until they are soft. Lift out and put with the rashers. Prepare the tomatoes. In a separate bowl, whisk the eggs and milk together and season with salt and pepper.

When the spaghetti is just 'bite' tender, drain it well. Melt the tablespoon of butter in the empty saucepan and put the spaghetti back in. Add in the rasher and vegetable mixture and stir together over a gentle heat. Then pour in the egg mixture. Cook over a gentle heat, tossing and stirring until barely cooked. Mix in the chopped fresh parsley. Serve immediately scattered with a little Parmesan, if liked.

CHRISTMAS SPAGHETTI

The Spaghetti Carbonara recipe is a good one to use for reheating turkey and ham. Instead of rashers, use **110 g (4 oz) each of turkey and ham.** Chop the meats and fry lightly (as the rashers) and make up as directed above.

Spanish Omelette (Q)

(Serves 4-5)

An ideal meal in a hurry! Like so many Mediterranean dishes, this contains lots of vegetables. Onions and potatoes and a little garlic are the main ingredients - but the variations are endless. The omelette is not folded but cooked on both sides either on a pan under the grill, or in the oven.

2-4 rashers, chopped
3-4 tablespoons oil (preferably olive)
2 large potatoes (about 225 g/8 oz) (see note)
1 large onion, chopped
2 cloves garlic, crushed or chopped
50-110 g (2-4 oz) mushrooms, chopped
½ small red pepper, chopped thinly (optional)
½ small courgette, chopped thinly
2-3 tomatoes, chopped
Salt and freshly ground black pepper
½ level teaspoon oregano
4 large eggs
4 tablespoons milk
A little grated cheese (optional)

A good sized frying pan.

Note: For best flavour, use raw potatoes, diced and fried. For speed, I sometimes use frozen chips, chopped! Cooked potatoes (left overs) are very handy though they will not be as crispy.

First fry the rashers in the oil until crispy. Lift out and fry the chopped potatoes until golden brown (and cooked through if using raw ones). Next add the chopped onion and fry until soft. Add in the garlic, mushrooms, pepper, courgette and tomatoes. Season with salt, pepper and oregano.

The pan will, by now, be nicely full of vegetables. Cook them gently until bite tender (about 5-10 minutes).

Meanwhile mix together the eggs and milk - don't make them too frothy. Season with salt and pepper. Pour into the pan on top of the vegetables. Shake the pan to mix through. Then cook over a moderate heat until fairly set. If heat is too high, the bottom will burn! Sprinkle with a little grated cheese and place under the grill to cook the top of the omelette to a lovely golden colour.

(Continued next page)

9

If you'd prefer not to turn on the grill - omit the cheese, slide the omelette right out onto a big plate and then turn it gently back onto the (oiled) pan and fry until golden underneath.

Serve hot or cold with salad.

OVEN BAKED SPAHISH OMELETTE
Serves (6 - 8)

When numbers are big, a frying pan is too small so it is necessary to bake the Spanish Omelette. I use a lasagne dish (about 30.5 x 23 cm/12" x 9") greased. Double the list of ingredients except the eggs, 6-7 large eggs will do.

Fry the rashers, potatoes, onion, garlic, mushrooms and courgettes, one at a time and transfer them to the dish. Add chopped pepper and tomatoes to the dish (without pre-frying). Season generously with salt, pepper and oregano. Mix the eggs and milk, season and pour into the dish. Scatter 75-110 g (3-4 oz) grated cheese over the top. Bake in a hot oven (200°C, 400°F, Gas 6) for about 35-45 minutes or until golden brown on top and set through.

Courgette Omelette (Q)

(Serves 1 or more)

Lightly fried, grated courgette, added to an omelette, gives it a lovely green speckled 'fresh' appearance. The quantities are for one omelette, increase as required.

25 g (1 oz) margarine or olive oil
110 g (4 oz) courgettes, washed
1 small clove garlic, crushed or chopped
Salt and freshly ground black pepper
⅛ teaspoon nutmeg
1 large egg (or 2 small eggs)
2 tablespoons milk

Melt half the margarine in a pan and grate the courgette directly into it. Add the garlic, salt, pepper and the nutmeg. Fry for a few minutes to soften.

Meanwhile, whisk the egg and milk together blending well but not making them too frothy. Add the courgette mixture from the pan and mix. Melt the remaining margarine in the pan and pour in the omelette mixture. Fry over a moderate heat. As mixture sets at the bottom, draw it in from the edge towards the centre of the pan (it gathers in, in 'wrinkles'). Let the runny mixture fill the empty spaces. Cook gently until omelette is golden brown underneath but still nice and moist (not runny) on top. Fold in two or three and turn out onto a plate.

Turkey and Chicken

Q = quick to cook   (F) = suitable for freezing

Turkey Pot Roast 12
Stuffed Roast Turkey Breast (F) **13**
Turkey and Ham Loaf (See Bacon Loaf) 59
Low Fat Creamy Chicken Breasts (Q) **14**
Saucy Chicken with Ginger (Q) **15**
Juicy Barbecue Sauce (Q) **16**
Chicken Joints in Juicy Barbecue Sauce 16
Chicken Joints in Orange Juice Sauce 17
Chicken Breasts in Orange Juice Sauce 18
Turkey in Orange Juice Sauce (Q) **18**
Chicken Joints in Sweet Barbecue Sauce 45
Chicken Stir-Fry with Pineapple (Q) **18**
Christmas (Turkey and Ham) Stir-Fry (Q) **19**
Chicken Stir-Fry with Tomato Juice (Q) **20**
Turkey Stir-Fry with Tomato Juice (Q) **21**
Chicken Stir-Fry with Apple Juice (Q) **49**
Cider Baked Chicken 21
Party Style Chicken Breasts with Mushrooms and White Wine 22
Chicken Lasagne (F) **23**
Chunky Chicken and Tomato Dish (Q) **44**

Chicken and turkey recipes are always great favourites. For something special try the Stuffed Roast Turkey Breast. The Saucy Chicken with Ginger is delicious, quick and ideal for small numbers. My recipe for Juicy Barbecue Sauce is a real winner as it can be cooked with chicken, meat or fish. To make a chicken stretch in a most tasty fashion, try the Chicken Lasagne - ideal for parties or long week-ends.

Chicken or turkey meat are nutritionally very good because of their low fat content and easy digestibility.

On the subject of fat, every fat is made up of individual fatty acids either saturated, polyunsaturated or monounsaturated. A certain amount of fat is essential in a healthy diet, the problem is not to eat too much!

Turkey Pot Roast

(Serves 6-10)

The small weekend turkeys are not as tasty as the big birds we get at Christmas time so I like to pot roast them. This has the added advantage of making the cooked turkey lovely and moist. Let me hastily explain that a large pot is not necessary. I use my roasting tin, completely covered in foil. If you wish the turkey can be stuffed.

1 turkey, 2.75 - 3.75 kg (6-8 lbs)
'Bed' of vegetables: 2 potatoes
2 sticks celery
2 carrots
1-2 onions
2 cloves garlic
Salt and freshly ground black pepper
1 level teaspoon mixed herbs
150 ml (¼ pt) turkey or chicken stock (use ½ cube if
necessary) OR use 150 ml (¼ pt) white wine
50 g (2 oz) butter or margarine

Cooking Time: Cook at a high temperature (220°C, 425°F, Gas 7) for 45 minutes then reduce heat (180°C, 350°F, Gas 4) and cook for another 1-1½ hours or until cooked through. An 8 lb turkey will take an extra ½ hour or so.

To prepare the turkey: It is a good idea to trim off the leg at the knee joint as it cuts the foil during cooking. Tie the two knees together - but not too tightly - say about 7.5 cm (3") apart. This keeps them from spreading out during cooking. If liked, stuff the breast cavity (see below).

To prepare the bed of vegetables: Wash and peel vegetables where necessary and chop them roughly. Mix them together and season them with salt and pepper and add the mixed herbs. Place them in a circle in the centre of the roasting tin.

To roast: Sit the turkey on top of the vegetables and pour in the stock. Spread butter generously over the breast and legs and season with salt and pepper. Cover the whole roasting tin with foil (no holes!) tucking it in under the rim all around the roasting tin. The aim is to prevent the delicious juices from escaping. Alternatively place the vegetables, stock and turkey in the same way - in a turkey roasting bag. Cook until tender.

To test if cooked: Waggle the legs - they should not be too rigid but rather loose. A second test is to squeeze the thigh meat (use a paper towel or two to protect your fingers from the heat) the flesh should be tender. Another way to check is to pierce the leg with a skewer, hold a spoon under it to catch the juices - if they are pink continue cooking - if clear or golden, turkey is cooked.

To stuff the turkey: The mushrooms and celery give a delicious flavour. I also prefer to use wholemeal breadcrumbs.

Turkey stuffing:
1 smallish onion, finely chopped
50 g (2 oz) margarine
2 cloves garlic, crushed or chopped
75 g (3 oz) mushrooms, chopped
110 g (4 oz) wholemeal (or white) breadcrumbs
1 stick celery, chopped finely
1 tablespoon chopped fresh parsley
1 teaspoon herbes de Provence (or mixed herbs)
Salt and freshly ground black pepper
4-6 tablespoons chicken or giblet stock (see note)

Note: Cook the turkey giblets (neck, liver etc.) in a saucepan with about 570 ml (1 pint) cold water. Also add an onion, carrot and stick of celery plus salt, pepper and ½ level teaspoon mixed herbs. Bring to the boil and simmer for about 30 minutes. Strain off stock. If liked, the chopped liver can be included in the stuffing. Use this stock for stuffing and for gravy.

Fry the onion in the margarine until soft and add the garlic. Add the mushrooms and fry to soften them. Take off the heat. Add the remaining ingredients to the pan and mix (if pan is too small, transfer to a bowl).

Place stuffing into the neck cavity. Fold skin over and round to back of the turkey, 'pin' closed with wooden cocktail sticks.

Stuffing Variation: Reduce mushrooms to 40 g (1½ oz) and instead use 50 g (2 oz) chopped cooking apple.

Stuffed Roast Turkey Breast (F)

(Serves 5-6)

This recipe gives wonderful flavour to a 'joint' of turkey breast. The breast is cut off the turkey in one piece.

1 'joint' turkey breast about 700-800g
(1½ - 1¾ lbs)
Stuffing as for Turkey Pot Roast (above)
A few strips of pork fat to cover the top of the breast
OR 1 packet streaky rashers

Cooking Time: Roast for about 45 minutes (200°C, 400°F, Gas 6) then reduce heat (180°C, 350°F, Gas 4) and cook for another 45-60 minutes.

Note: Sometimes half turkey breast 'joints' are available - use half amount of stuffing. Cooking time will be about 45 mins - 1 hour in total.

The breast has a natural division like a 'pocket' (almost like two fillets of breast), cut with a sharp knife to make this 'pocket' even bigger. Put the stuffing into the pocket. (You may have a tiny bit left over). Sit the joint on a foil lined tin. Cover the top completely with pork fat or rashers, if possible tucking them right down the sides. Fold the foil over the whole lot and roast in the oven until cooked through. Turn back foil for the last 15-20 minutes of cooking. To test, pierce with a skewer, it should be tender.

Serve hot with gravy or cold with salad. (Can be frozen with the cooking juices spooned over it.)

Low Fat Creamy Chicken Breasts (Q)

(Serves 4)

Chicken breasts (despite their price!) are very handy for a fast meal. Because of their low fat content, it seems a pity to 'bung' them on a pan and fry them. This method uses skimmed milk to cook them.

4 skinless chicken breast fillets
275 ml (½ pt) skimmed milk (see note)
¼-½ chicken stock cube
175 g (6 oz) mushrooms, sliced
1-2 cloves garlic, crushed or chopped
2 rounded teaspoons cornflour
Salt and freshly ground black or white pepper

Note: Fresh (full fat) milk can be used if you are not watching the fat content.

If chicken breasts are rather thick, slit them in two. Put the chicken breasts into a saucepan with the milk and the piece of stock cube. Put in the mushrooms and garlic. Bring to the boil and then simmer very gently with the lid on until chicken breasts are cooked (about 15 minutes). Lift the chicken breasts out of the saucepan and keep warm. (Don't worry if the milk has a grainy look).

Blend the cornflour with a little water and add to the saucepan. Bring to the boil, stirring, to thicken. Season to taste with salt and pepper. (If white peppercorns are available, use them rather than the black because of the whitish colour of this dish). Pour sauce over the chicken. Serve hot. Accompany with vegetables of your choice or simply with crusty bread and a salad.

Saucy Chicken with Ginger (Q)

(Serves 2)

Don't let the name put you off! The combination of ingredients is wonderful and quick to cook. The sauce has a slightly sweet, tart taste with the subtle flavour of the lovely fresh ginger. Do try it.

1 medium onion, chopped
2 tablespoons oil
1-2 cloves garlic, crushed or chopped
2 skinless chicken breast fillets
2 sticks celery
170 ml (⅓ pt) apple juice
1 level teaspoon cornflour
2 tablespoons mayonnaise
2 teaspoons grated fresh root ginger
Salt and freshly ground black pepper

To Serve:
Chopped fresh chives

Fry the onion in the oil until soft and add in the garlic. Add the chicken and celery and fry until the chicken turns white or light golden. Blend the apple juice into the cornflour and stir in the mayonnaise, grated ginger, salt and pepper. (It may be necessary to use a whisk to blend in the mayonnaise). Add this liquid to the pan and bring gently to the boil. Simmer with the lid on for about 10 minutes or until the chicken is cooked.

Serve scattered with chopped chives.

REHEATING If adding leftover cooked meat to a sauce to reheat it - it is most important to bring the sauce to the boil and to boil gently for a few minutes to ensure ALL the meat is heated to boiling point. This ensures that any harmful bacteria will be 'killed'. This is especially important with chicken.

Reheating in a microwave - reheat food to piping hot and let it cool sufficiently to eat. Heating only to eating temperature is not enough. This applies especially to chicken, meat, fish and egg dishes.

Juicy Barbecue Sauce (Q)

This is a fabulous sauce - it is so adaptable. Its sharp, sweet taste adds great flavour to many dishes. Try it with fish. It can also be served as an accompanying sauce e.g. with roast chicken.

1 medium onion, chopped
25 g (1 oz) margarine
2-3 cloves garlic, crushed or chopped
1 level tablespoon cornflour
275-425 ml (½-¾ pint) water
1 chicken stock cube
2 tablespoons tomato purée
1-2 tablespoons brown sugar (demerara)
1-2 tablespoons chutney (preferably Mango)
Salt and freshly ground black pepper
¼ level teaspoon cayenne pepper
1 teaspoon mustard

Fry the onion in the margarine until soft, then add in the garlic. Blend together the cornflour and water and add to the onion along with the chicken stock cube. Stir in the tomato purée, brown sugar, chutney, salt, pepper, cayenne pepper (hot!) and mustard. Bring the sauce mixture to the boil stirring all the time. Simmer gently for a few minutes. Then serve or use as required.

Chicken Joints in Juicy Barbecue Sauce

(Serves 4-6)

Trays of assorted chicken joints are often available at quite a good price. These pieces are usually of the leg and wing variety which are not the most popular with some members of my family! Cooking them in the **Juicy Barbecue Sauce** makes all the difference!

Brown the outside of the chicken pieces by frying them in a little fat or oil. Place them in a single layer close together in an ovenproof dish or tin. Pour the sauce over them and cover with a piece of foil (it needn't be too well covered). Cook in the oven until meat is tender — about 50-60 minutes (190°C, 375°F, gas 5). Serve in the juicy sauce.

Pork Chops in Juicy Barbecue Sauce

(Serves 4-6)

Pork chops (4-6) are very tasty cooked in the same way as the Chicken in Juicy Barbecue Sauce (page 16). First trim off excess fat and then fry in a little oil to brown each side. Place them in a single layer, cover with the sauce and cook covered with foil. They take about the same length of time as the chicken.

Fish in Juicy Barbecue Sauce (Q)

(Serves 4)

Use recipe for Chicken in Juicy Barbecue Sauce (page 16), omit chicken and use fish.

Thick fillets of cod, salmon or trout (4 x 150 g (5 oz) each) are also really good cooked in this sauce. No need to brown them, just place in an ovenproof dish in a single layer, cover them with sauce and cook as for the chicken. They will be cooked in about 20 minutes (if the sauce is hot when poured over them).

Chicken Joints in Orange Juice Sauce

(serves 4-6)

This simple fresh Orange Juice Sauce gives an excellent flavour to baked chicken joints.

Orange Juice Sauce:
25 g (1 oz) margarine
1 large onion, thinly sliced
1-2 cloves garlic, crushed or chopped
Juice 2-3 oranges
225 ml (8 fl oz) water
1 chicken stock cube
1 level teaspoon cinnamon
1 level teaspoon oregano
1 tablespoon chutney (preferably Mango)
Salt and freshly ground black pepper
1 rounded tablespoon cornflour (blended with a little water)

Also:
4-6 joints of chicken (the bones in the chicken add great flavour)

Cooking Time: About 60 minutes (190°C, 375°F, Gas 5).

Melt the margarine in a pan or saucepan and fry the onion until soft, then add in the garlic. Then add in all the remaining sauce ingredients. Bring to the boil.

Place the chicken joints side by side in an ovenproof dish. Pour the sauce over them. Cover well with foil and cook until chicken is cooked. Spoon off any fat that comes to the surface.

Serve scattered with chopped fresh parsley.

Chicken Breasts in Orange Juice Sauce (Q)

Skinless chicken breast fillets can also be simmered in a saucepan in Orange Juice Sauce until cooked. Use **4-6 chicken breasts.** If liked, brown them in a little margarine before adding to the sauce. Bring to the boil and simmer gently until cooked through (about 20 minutes).

Turkey in Orange Juice Sauce (Q)

Left over turkey slices can be reheated in this tasty orange juice sauce. Use about **350-450 g (¾-1 lb) cooked turkey.** Bring to the boil in the sauce and simmer for 5-10 minutes.

Chicken Stir-Fry with Pineapple (Q)

(Serves 4-5)

A most popular recipe with my family! The pineapple is excellent with the other ingredients.

1 small onion, thinly sliced
1-2 cloves garlic, crushed
50-75 g (2-3 oz) sweetcorn (thawed)
1 red or yellow pepper, cut in strips
110 g (4 oz) mushrooms, sliced
50-110 g (2-4 oz) mangetout, cut in short lengths
3 tablespoons pineapple chunks
1 teaspoon grated fresh root ginger (optional)
3 skinless chicken breast fillets

Sauce:
150 ml (¼ pt) pineapple juice (from tin of pineapple)
2-3 tablespoons soy sauce
1 heaped teaspoon cornflour
Salt and freshly ground black pepper

To fry:
2-4 tablespoons of oil

Before you start, have all the vegetables prepared. Also cut the chicken breast fillets into narrow finger-like strips. Have the sauce ingredients ready - simply mix them together in a jug or bowl.

Heat the oil in a wok or large frying pan (or a wide saucepan). Fry the chicken pieces until they are golden brown all over. Lift out and keep warm near the cooker. Put the onion into the wok along with all the other vegetables. Fry them, tossing constantly over the heat until half tender. Then add in the pineapple and the grated ginger, return the fried chicken pieces to the wok. Also add in the sauce mixture.

Bring to the boil, constantly stirring everything together until sauce thickens, the vegetables are bite tender and the chicken is cooked through. (Cut the thickest piece of chicken in half to check).

Serve with rice or noodles.

Pork Stir-Fry with Pineapple (Q)

(Serves 4)

A **pork steak (350 g/12 oz)** can be used instead of chicken breasts in the above recipe. Cut the pork steak into thin slices, then cut each slice in half. Make up as directed.

Christmas (Turkey and Ham) Stir-Fry (Q)

(Serves 4-6)

An ideal way to use Christmas leftovers. Use **225 g (8 oz) each of cooked turkey and cooked ham** instead of the chicken breasts in the above recipe. Cut these into fingerlike strips. Fry them in some of the oil in the wok. When lightly golden, lift out and keep warm. Make the stir-fry as directed.

Chicken Stir-Fry with Tomato Juice (Q)

(Serves 4-5)

The tomato juice for this recipe is the kind you buy in a carton or jar (like orange juice). The little bit of chilli powder gives a nice 'kick'.

1 small onion, thinly sliced
1 leek, washed and sliced
OR 2-3 spring onions (scallions) sliced
2 sticks celery, sliced thinly
½ red pepper, cut in short narrow pieces
Half of a 225 g (8 oz) tin water chestnuts, drained and
sliced (optional) (See note)
50 g (2 oz) peas (defrosted)
3 skinless chicken breast fillets
2-4 tablespoons oil

Sauce:
150 ml (¼ pt) tomato juice
2-3 tablespoons soy sauce
½ chicken stock cube (optional)
Salt and freshly ground black pepper
¼ teaspoon chilli pepper (or cayenne pepper)
2-3 teaspoons vinegar
1 teaspoon sugar
1 heaped teaspoon cornflour

Note: Tinned water chestnuts make a lovely addition to a stir fry because of their crisp texture. Their flavour is very mild (remainder of tin can be frozen).

Before you start, have all the vegetables prepared. Also cut the chicken breasts into small pieces. Mix the sauce ingredients together in a jug or bowl.

Fry the chicken pieces in the hot oil in a wok (or good sized frying pan or saucepan). When golden brown and just cooked, lift out and keep warm near cooker. Add the vegetables to the wok and fry, tossing constantly until half tender. Then add back the chicken and pour in the sauce ingredients. Bring to the boil, constantly stirring everything together until sauce thickens and the vegetables are bite tender. To be sure the chicken is cooked, cut the thickest piece in half to see the centre.

Serve with rice or noodles.

Pork Stir-Fry with Tomato Juice (Q)

(Serves 4)

A **Pork Steak (350 g/12 oz)** can be used instead of the chicken breasts in the previous recipe. Cut into thin slices and cut each one in half.

Turkey Stir-Fry with Tomato Juice (Q)

(Serves 4-5)

Sliced raw turkey breast can be used instead of the chicken in the Chicken Stir-Fry with Tomato Juice recipe. Use **350-450 g (¾-1 lb) of turkey breast escalopes.**

Cider Baked Chicken

(Serves 5-6)

A sort of a casserole. The cider gives a lovely flavour.

1 full chicken or 5-10 chicken joints
2 tablespoons oil
1 onion, chopped
1-2 cloves garlic, crushed or chopped
3-4 tomatoes, skinned and quartered
2 sticks celery, chopped
275 ml (½ pt) cider
Salt and freshly ground black pepper
1 level teaspoon mixed herbs
2 rounded teaspoons cornflour

To serve:
Chopped fresh parsley

Cooking Time: About 1½ hours (190°C, 375°F, Gas 5). Joints take a little less time (about 1 hour). Reduce heat after 45 minutes (180°C, 350°F, Gas 4) if it is doing nicely.

Fry the whole chicken (as best you can!) in the oil to brown the outside. If using joints, do the same. Transfer to a casserole.
Fry the onion and garlic to soften it, then add to the chicken with all the remaining ingredients, except the cornflour. Cover and bake until cooked through.

Pour off the cooking juices into a saucepan. Drop in 4-5 cubes of ice to sort of 'set' the fat that rises to the surface so you can easily remove it (save it for frying something another day). Blend the cornflour with a little water and add it in. Bring to the boil, stirring to thicken. Pour back over chicken. (If whole chicken has been cooked, it can be cut up into serving sections, put back into sauce to reheat and serve).

Serve scattered with chopped parsley.

Party Style Chicken Breasts with Mushrooms and White Wine

(Serves 8)

This creamy sauce gives a wonderful flavour to chicken breasts. It has the added advantage that it can be prepared the day before and reheated.

8-12 skinless chicken breast fillets (see note)
75 g (3 oz) margarine
1 medium onion
2-3 cloves garlic, crushed or chopped
450 g (1 lb) mushrooms sliced
½ litre (¾ pt) white wine (NOT a sweet wine)
1 chicken stock cube
275 ml (½ pt) water
Salt and freshly ground black (or white) pepper
1 level teaspoon herbes de Provence (or mixed herbs)
50 g (2 oz) margarine or butter) ⎫ to make kneaded
50 g (2 oz) flour ⎬ butter
¼ teaspoon nutmeg
Juice ½ lemon
75 ml (3 fl oz) fresh cream (optional)

Note: Correctly speaking, 1 chicken breast fillet is sufficient for 1 serving, but for a party it is better to err on the generous side!

Fry the chicken breasts in the margarine until golden brown on each side. Transfer to a large saucepan. Next fry the onion until soft and add the garlic. Lift out with slotted spoon and put with the chicken breasts. Fry the sliced mushrooms in the pan until they are a nice golden colour - do this in two to three lots depending on the size of your pan. Add them to the chicken breasts along with the wine, stock cube, water, salt, pepper and the herbs.

Cover with a lid, bring to the boil and then simmer very gently until the chicken is tender. Ideally, allow to cool at this stage because any excess fat will rise to the surface and can be removed.

To thicken sauce: Mash together the 50 g (2 oz) margarine and the 50 g (2 oz) flour to make a paste called Kneaded Butter. Lift the chicken breasts out of the saucepan, (the mushrooms can be left in the saucepan). Bring the contents of the saucepan to the boil and drop in little teaspoons of the kneaded butter. Use a whisk to mix thoroughly. When sauce is thick enough, flavour with more salt and pepper if necessary. Also add nutmeg, lemon juice and cream. Replace the chicken breasts. Keep covered in a cool place (even overnight) and reheat when ready to serve.

When reheating - bring slowly to the boil and simmer gently but thoroughly to be sure the chicken is heated to piping hot.

Chicken Lasagne (F)

(Serves 8)

A delicious way to serve a chicken! The sauce is made using stock from the cooked chicken. (It is very handy if you can cook the chicken the day before.) Great for parties or cooking ahead for long weekends.

To cook chicken:
1 medium chicken
1.4 litres (2½ pts) water
2-3 cloves garlic
1 onion, 1 carrot, 1 stick celery
1 level teaspoon herbes de Provence (or mixed herbs)
1 chicken stock cube
Salt and freshly ground black pepper

Mushroom layer:
350 g (12 oz) mushrooms, sliced
2-3 tablespoons oil
1-2 cloves garlic, crushed
175 g (6 oz) courgettes, grated
⅛ teaspoon nutmeg
salt and freshly ground black pepper
1 heaped teaspoon cornflour
A little cold water (50 ml/2 fl oz)

Variations: Substitute the courgettes with extra mushrooms, especially if planning to freeze lasagne.

Sauce:
1 litre (1¾ pts) stock, from the cooked chicken (See note)
175 g (6 oz) margarine
175 g (6 oz) flour
175 ml(6 fl oz) milk (reduce with this)
1 teaspoon grainy mustard
2-3 tablespoons lemon juice

Also: 9-12 pieces (sheets) of lasagne. Choose lasagne that requires no pre-cooking.

Note: 275 ml (½ pt) white wine can be used instead of 275 ml (½ pt) of the stock.

Lasagne Dish: About 30.5 cm x 23 cm (12" x 9").

Cooking Time: Bake for about 45-60 minutes (190°C, 375°F, Gas 5). If the lasagne is baked immediately after assembling while the sauce is still warm, it cooks in the shorter time.

Step I: Cook the chicken. Put the chicken in the water with the garlic, onion, carrot, celery, herbs, stock cube, salt and pepper. Bring to the boil and then simmer gently with the lid on for about 1-1¼ hours until tender.

Remove all the flesh from the bones and chop it roughly (discarding the skin and bones). There should be about 450-550 g (1-1¼ lbs) of cooked chicken. Strain off 1 litre (1¾ pts) of the cooking liquid and use for the sauce.

Step 2: The mushroom layer. Lightly fry the mushrooms in the oil until soft. Add in the garlic. Then add in the grated courgettes, the nutmeg, salt and pepper and the cornflour blended with a little cold water. Bring to the boil.

Step 3: To make the sauce (lots of sauce is required!). Put the strained stock (and wine) into a big saucepan. Add in the margarine (cut into lumps) and the flour. Use a whisk and stir briskly over the heat bringing slowly to the boil, by which time it will be a nice creamy sauce. Stir in the milk, and flavour with the mustard, lemon juice and salt and pepper if necessary.

Step 4: Count out the sheets of lasagne! You need enough to make three layers in the lasagne dish. (The thinner the lasagne the better, then it doesn't absorb too much sauce.)

Step 5: To assemble the lasagne. Spread about 150 ml (¼ pt) of the sauce over the base of the dish. Cover that with a layer of lasagne sheets, laid side by side (break sheets to fit, if necessary). Now spread out all the chopped chicken meat in one layer. Cover it with 275 ml (½ pt) of the sauce.

The second layer of lasagne sheets is now laid out, side by side. Next, spread out the mushroom and courgettes layer and cover it with another 275 ml (½ pt) of the sauce. The final layer of lasagne sheets is now put in place and the remaining 425 ml (¾ pt) of the sauce is poured over the top.

Bake until golden brown and bubbling all over. If by chance any melted fat rises to the surface, use paper kitchen towels to soak it away. Leave to stand for 10-15 minutes before serving. (If made in advance and stored in fridge, warm up in kitchen before cooking).

FISH

(Q) = quick to cook   (F) = suitable for freezing

Trout with Mushrooms (Q) **26**
Plaice with Mushrooms (Q) **26**
Stuffing Topped Cod (or Salmon) (Q) **27**
Fish Italian Style (Q) **28**
Rolled Fillets of Plaice (Q) **29**
Sauce Marie Rose (Q) **29**
Salmon with Soy Sauce and Ginger (Q) **29**
Fish Pastry Parcels 30
Fish 'n' Pasta Dish (Q) **31**
Fish in Juicy Barbecue Sauce 17
Mussels (Q) **32**
Mussels with Pasta (Q) **32**
Crunchy Tuna and Cottage Cheese Salad (Q) **33**
Pasta with Tomato and Shrimp Sauce (Q) **34**
Smoked Trout Cheesecake 34
Smoked Mackerel Quiche (F) **36**
Smoked Salmon Quiche (F) **37**
Hot Tomatoes Stuffed with Tuna 38
Mackerel in Apple Juice Sauce (Q) **59**

Fish is supported by water and so its muscles are much more tender than land animals. They are easy to digest and quick to cook. Surveys have shows that the inclusion of oily fish (salmon, mackerel, tuna etc.) in the diet has a beneficial effect on our health. Fish oils contain certain fatty acids that are exclusive to them.

Try the lovely Stuffing Topped Cod (or Salmon) or the Fish Pastry Parcels - for tasty ways to make the most of fish. For absolute speed and a delicious crunch try a light meal of Crunchy Tuna and Cottage Cheese Salad.

Trout with Mushrooms (Q)

(Serves 3-4)

Large fillets of trout topped with a mushroom mixture can be cooked in the pan or in the oven. Dill weed (optional) blends well with mushrooms and fish.

Mushroom Mixture:
1-2 tablespoons oil
1 medium onion, chopped finely
2 cloves garlic, crushed or chopped
225 g (8 oz) mushrooms, chopped finely
Salt and freshly ground black pepper
½ level teaspoon dill weed (or mixed herbs)
2-3 tablespoons lemon juice

Fish:
450 g (1 lb) trout fillet(s)

Cooking time: About 25-35 minutes in oven (190°C, 375°F, Gas 5) OR cook in a frying pan.

Heat the oil and fry the onion until soft. Add in the garlic and mushrooms. Continue to fry until mushrooms are soft and reduced in volume. Flavour with salt, pepper, dill and lemon juice.

Place the fish on a greased tin or ovenproof dish. Spoon the mushroom mixture directly on top of fish. Spread out to cover the fish. Cover loosely with foil and bake until cooked.

To cook in the pan: After making the mushroom mixture, lift it out of the pan. Place the fish in the pan (oiled) and cover with the mushroom mixture. Cover pan with a lid or foil and cook gently until fish is cooked through, about 15-20 minutes.

Variation: Stir a few tablespoons of cream or natural yogurt into the mushroom mixture before putting on the fish.

Plaice with Mushrooms (Q)

Plaice is also excellent cooked in this way. Use **450 g (1 lb) fillets of plaice.**

Stuffing Topped Cod (or Salmon) (Q)

(Serves 4)

This tasty stuffing makes a delicious meal of fillet(s) of fish. Choose cod or farmed salmon - or indeed any fish fillets of your choice. Use one large fillet or individual portion fillets.

450-550 g (1-1¼ lb) fish fillets (see note)

Stuffing:
50 g (2 oz) margarine
1 medium onion, finely chopped
1-2 sticks celery, finely chopped
1 small cooking apple (about 225 g/8 oz)
1-2 cloves garlic, crushed or chopped
50 g (2 oz) breadcrumbs (preferably wholemeal)
1 tablespoon chopped parsley
½ chicken stock cube (optional)
Juice ½ orange OR water
A little melted margarine or oil

Note: Nicest if fillets are not too thin.

Cooking Time: About 25-35 minutes (190°C, 375°F, Gas 5).

Place the fillet(s) of fish on a greased ovenproof dish (or tin). Melt the margarine in a frying pan. Add the onion and cook until soft. Add in the celery and the peeled chopped cooking apple along with the garlic. Next stir in the breadcrumbs and parsely and mix. If using the chicken stock cube, mash it up in the orange juice and add only enough to the stuffing mixture in the pan to make it moist but not sloppy. Put the stuffing on top of the fish and spread out to completely cover the fish. Dribble the melted margarine or oil over the top.

Cook until stuffing is nice and crispy on top and fish is cooked through.

Serve decorated with slices of lemon.

Fish Italian Style (Q)

(Serves 3-4)

Take a piece of cod to a new level with this delicious Mediterranean style recipe.

450 g (1 lb) cod fillets
1 onion, chopped
2-3 tablespoons olive oil (approx)
1 clove garlic, crushed or chopped
110 g (4 oz) mushrooms, sliced
175 g (6 oz) courgette, chopped
Salt and freshly ground black pepper
¼ teaspoon nutmeg
½ level teaspoon oregano (or mixed herbs)
Tin of chopped tomatoes
75 g (3 oz) grated cheese (mixture of cheddar and
mozzarella) (optional)

Cooking Time: About 30 minutes (200°C, 400°F, Gas 6).

Place the fish in an ovenproof dish, arranging pieces in a single layer. Next fry the onion in the olive oil until soft and add the garlic. Fry for a minute or two, then put the mushrooms into the pan and the courgettes. Fry a little before scattering over the fish. Season with salt and pepper and flavour with nutmeg and oregano. Spread the tin of tomatoes over everything, season again with a little salt and pepper.

Bake in the oven for about 15 minutes, then scatter the cheese over the top. Return to the oven for another 15 mintues or until cheese melts and browns lightly.

Frying pan method: Instead of placing fish in ovenproof dish, place in a second frying pan over a gentle heat. As the onions, mushrooms etc. are fried, scatter them over the fish in the same way. Finally heat the tin of chopped tomatoes in the first frying pan before pouring over the fish and vegetables. Cover with a lid and simmer gently until fish is cooked, about 15-20 minutes. Scatter with cheese and brown under a grill.

Serve with vegetables or with a salad and crusty bread.

Note: **To skin fish fillets.** *Place the fish, skin side down on a board with the narrow end (or a corner) facing you. Insert a sharp knife between the flesh and the skin. Hold the skin tightly with your other hand. The blade of the knife will be facing away from you. Continue to cut, keeping the blade of the knife slightly slanted downwards towards the skin until all is removed, the skin is quite tough and won't cut easily. Otherwise ask your fishmonger to do it!*

Anti-clockwise: Meatloaf; Baked courgettes; Summer medley; French fruit flan;
Wholemeal herb and cheese scones; Spare ribs; Fresh fruit salad

Christmas turkey and ham stir-fry

Pot roast of beef

Rhubarb compôte (stewed)

Rolled Fillets of Plaice (Q)

(Serves 1 or more)

A most succulent way to cook plaice.

1 fillet plaice per person
Salt and freshly ground black pepper
2-3 teaspoons mayonnaise

Cooking Time: About 15-20 minutes (200°C, 400°F, Gas 6)

Remove the skin from the plaice (ask your fishmonger or see page 28 for directions). Place fillet of fish skinned side upwards; spread half of the mayonnaise over the fish, season with salt and pepper and roll up. (The skinned side is inside the roll.) Spread the remaining mayonnaise on top. Place in greased dish, cover loosely with foil and bake until cooked through.

Serve hot, or serve cold with sauce Marie Rose.

Sauce Maire Rose (Q)

8 tablespoons mayonnaise
3 tablespoons tomato ketchup
½ teaspoon Worcester sauce or Soy sauce

Simply mix these together and serve on prawn cocktail or with fish salads.

Salmon with Soy Sauce and Ginger (Q)

(Serves 2 or more)

Fresh root ginger is not something you'd automatically associate with fish - but it is excellent. Fresh root ginger is one of those ingredients that once you start using it, you will wonder where else you can include it!

2 salmon cutlets or 2 serving sized fillets
1-2 tablespoons oil (preferably olive oil)
4 mushrooms, chopped
4 spring onions (scallions), thinly sliced
2 teaspoons grated fresh root ginger
1-2 tablespoons soy sauce (see note)
Salt and freshly ground black pepper

Note: If you have a choice of soy sauce, choose a light one.

Fry the salmon on each side to brown it lightly. Then add in all the other ingredients. Cover with a lid (or foil) and simmer gently. Stir ocasionally and spoon some of the mixture over the salmon until cooked through, takes about 8-10 minutes.

Flavours mingle better when fish is cooked in a pan rather than being grilled. If watching calories, use a non stick pan so minimal oil will do!

Fish Pastry Parcels

(Serves 4)

This makes a very satisfying meal from an 'adequate' portion of fish. All you need is a tossed salad to serve with it - or vegetables of your choice.

1 packet frozen puff pastry (375 g/13 oz) (see note)
450 g (1 lb) fillets of thickish white fish (cod, haddock etc.)
1 onion, finely chopped
2 tablespoons oil
175 g (6 oz) mushrooms, chopped
1-2 cloves garlic
Salt and freshly ground black pepper
4 teaspoons lemon juice
4 heaped teaspoons mayonnaise

Cooking Time: 25-35 minutes (200°C, 400°F, Gas 6).

Note: A packet of ready rolled puff pastry (375 g/13 oz) is very convenient for this recipe.

Cut the packet of pastry in two and roll out each piece into a square (25.5 cm/10"). Then cut each square in four. Put four squares on a greased baking tin.

Skin the fish (see page 28) and divide into 4 even portions; place each portion onto a square of pastry (on the tin).

Fry the onion in the oil until soft. Add in the mushrooms and garlic and fry until soft and reduced in volume. Season with salt and pepper. Spoon over the four portions of fish. Place a spoon of lemon juice and mayonnaise on top of each portion. Wet the edges of the pastry on which the fish filling is sitting. Slightly stretch the centre of each remaining piece of pastry so that it will fit over the 'bulge' of the filling. Place on top and press edges very

30

well to seal, trim the edges. Pierce the top in 2-3 places with the point of a knife. Place on a greased baking tin or oven proof plate and bake in the oven until a good golden brown colour.

Serve with a salad or vegetables of your choice.

Fish 'n' Pasta Dish (Q)

(Serves 4-5)

A lovely family dish. The fish is cooked in milk which is used to make the sauce. Then the fish and pasta are mixed through the sauce and grilled, making the top lovely and crispy.

175 g (6 oz) pasta shapes (shells or twists etc.)
1 fish or chicken stock cube
450 g (1 lb) cod fillets
570 ml (1 pt) milk
175 g (6 oz) thinly sliced mushrooms
Salt and freshly ground black pepper
2 heaped teaspoons cornflour (blended with a little water)
110 g (4 oz) frozen peas
110 g (4 oz) frozen sweet corn
25 g (1 oz) grated cheddar cheese

Cook the pasta in boiling water to which the stock cube has been added for flavour. When just tender, drain well. Meanwhile, cook/poach the cod in the milk in a good sized saucepan along with the mushrooms. Season with salt and pepper. Lift out the fish when it is cooked. Break it into chunks and remove skin and bones.

Add the blended cornflour to the milk and mushrooms, also add in the peas and corn and simmer gently for 3-5 minutes stirring to thicken the sauce and cook the vegetables. Next add the chunks of fish and the drained pasta into the sauce. Stir gently but thoroughly and pour into greased hot ovenproof dish. Scatter the cheese over the top, cook under a moderate grill until top is golden and crispy.

In oven: If dish has been prepared in advance, it can be reheated in the oven, 190°C, 375°F, Gas 5, for about 30-45 minutes until heated through and top is crispy and golden.

Mussels (Q)

Fresh mussels have a truly delicious flavour. Even though they may not be a regular item on your shopping list give yourself a treat. Mussels are available all year round but are particularly good in the cooler months (October to March).

It is very important that mussels are fresh so buy from a reliable fishmonger. They will keep in a damp container in the fridge for 2-3 days - but it is better to use them as soon as possible.

Mussels must be alive which is easily judged as the shells will be tightly closed or they will close tightly when tapped. If they don't tighten - throw them out. If shells are broken throw them out. Never take a chance with mussels (or indeed any shellfish). Wash mussels in several changes of cold water. If any of the mussels float to the top of the water - throw them out. After washing drain them and cut away the stringy bits (beard) from the shells.

To cook mussels:

Allow about **450 g (1 lb) of mussels** per person for a main dish or half that for a starter. Place the prepared mussels into a wide dry saucepan. Cover with the lid (there is no need to add any liquid). Cook over a low heat until the mussels are open. This takes about 3-5 minutes or so.

To serve:

Take off the top half of the shell, leaving the mussels in the lower half. Serve in wide soup bowls or plates and sprinkle with **garlic flavoured melted butter,** mixed with a little of the cooking juices. Serve with crusty bread (and wine!).

Variation: When cooking the mussels, instead of using a dry saucepan put in 1 glass of white wine, 2-3 cloves crushed garlic and a small knob of butter.

Mussels with Pasta (Q)

(Serves 2-4)

These flavours blend wonderfully. This amount will serve two as a main dish and four as a starter.

225 g (8 oz) pasta, twirls or shells
1 chicken or fish stock cube
450 g (1 lb) fresh mussels
15 g (½ oz) butter

2 cloves garlic, crushed
175 ml (6 fl oz) fresh cream
Salt and freshly ground black pepper
Tablespoon chopped fresh parsley

Cook the pasta in boiling salted water, to which you add the stock cube, until just tender. Drain thoroughly.

Meanwhile cook the mussels as described in previous recipe. Then remove them from their shells.

Melt the butter and add the garlic. Stir in the cream. Season with salt and pepper. Add in the pasta and mussels.

Toss together and sprinkle parsley over.

Crunchy Tuna and Cottage Cheese Salad (Q)

(Serves 2-3)

Hold on a second! Even if you dislike cottage cheese, I bet you'll love this recipe. The peanuts, celery and apple included make this deliciously crunchy. Serve with lettuce or in pitta pockets.

1 tin (100 g) tuna fish, drained
1 carton (225 g/8 oz) cottage cheese (choose a garlic and
herbs OR chives flavour)
2 sticks celery, chopped finely
1 eating apple, chopped finely
50 g (2 oz) salted peanuts

Mix all the ingredients together in a bowl. Serve on plates with lettuce or in toasted pitta pockets.

One way I use to combat my desire for sweet, high calorie foods is to include an element of sweetness in my main dish. The Chinese do this too, desserts hardly feature in true Chinese cuisine.

Pasta with Tomato and Shrimp Sauce (Q)

(Serves 3-4)

A lovely fresh tasting dish quite low in calories. Very quick to prepare. The cayenne pepper gives a gentle "kick" to the flavour.

225-350 g (8-12 oz) spaghetti or other pasta shape
(e.g. shells)
1 chicken stock or fish stock cube
½ small onion, chopped
1 tablespoon oil
1 clove garlic, crushed
1 tin chopped tomatoes
1 tin shrimps (185 g/6½ oz) (drained)
50 g (2 oz) each frozen peas and sweetcorn
1 tablespoon chopped parsley
Salt and freshly ground black pepper
¼ teaspoon cayenne pepper
½ teaspoon oregano
1 teaspoon sugar
1 heaped teaspoon cornflour

To serve: chopped parsley

Cook the pasta in boiling water to which the stock cube is added. When cooked to 'bite' tenderness, drain thoroughly.

Meanwhile as the pasta cooks, prepare the sauce: In a saucepan, first fry the onion in the oil until soft, then add the garlic. Next add in the tomatoes, the shrimps, the peas and the sweetcorn. Add the parsley and season with salt and pepper. Flavour with the cayenne pepper, the oregano and sugar. Add the cornflour blended with a little water. Heat everything to boiling point, stirring, and simmer for a few minutes.

Serve poured over the pasta. Scatter parsley on top.

Smoked Trout Cheesecake

(Serves 5-8)

If you are puzzled at the idea of a smoked trout cheesecake, let me hasten to explain that it makes a delightful light summer meal. It is equally good served as a starter. The finished cheesecake is quite shallow compared to the more usual dessert type cheesecakes, but the balance is just right.

Base:
150 g (5 oz) salty crackers (e.g. wheat germ crackers)
75 g (3 oz) melted butter or margarine

Cheese and trout mixture:
Juice of 1 large lemon
Water
1 sachet of gelatine
1 carton (225 g/8 oz) cottage cheese (natural)
1 packet (200 g/7 oz) cream cheese
(preferably 'light'/low fat)
1 tablespoon mayonnaise (optional)
175 g (6 oz) skinless fillet of smoked trout
Freshly ground black pepper
A little salt (if necessary)

Tin: Round tin 23 cm (9") diameter with removable base, oiled lightly.

Prepare the base: Crush the crackers into fine crumbs and mix with the melted butter. Spread evenly over the base of the tin. Press down well. Chill in the fridge so the crumbs will 'set'.

Cheese and trout mixture: Add just enough water to the lemon juice to measure 150 ml (¼ pt). Bring to the boil - immediately remove from the heat and sprinkle in the gelatine. Stir to dissolve completely. If necessary reheat slightly but don't let it boil again. Allow to cool completely.

Empty the cottage cheese into a food processor along with the cream cheese. 'Buzz' to make a smooth mix Then add the mayonnaise and the trout (be sure there are no bones) and 'buzz' to mix. Season with pepper and just a small bit of salt. Mix the gelatine mixture through this.

If no food processor is available - press the cottage cheese through a sieve to smooth out the lumps. Mash the smoked trout, then mix all the ingredients together. Pour mixture into the prepared tin and chill for a few hours. Loosen from the edges of the tin with a knife and lift out. Serve decorated with lemon slices, and mustard cress.

To serve as a starter: Cut in slim wedges and serve on individual plates. Decorate with slice or twist of lemon, mustard cress and a leaf of lettuce.

Boiling destroys the setting quality of gelatine.

Smoked Mackerel Quiche (F)

(Serves 5-6)

Smoked mackerel is delicious in a quiche. If you don't believe me - just try it! Somehow the eggs and milk used in the ingredients seem to 'round off' the flavour of the smoked mackerel - which I personally find too strong to eat just on its own. Vaccuum packs of smoked mackerel are very reasonably priced and they keep well in the fridge.

The Pastry base: You can use frozen pastry, either shortcrust or puff. The whole packet (usually about 375 g/13 oz) is too much for one quiche and not enough for two - I usually make a few little jam tarts or mince pies with the extra bit! If you'd prefer to make your own, I recommend my delicious Brown Shortcrust Pastry. This pastry can be used immediately after it is made. It needs no 'rest' in the fridge.

75 g (3 oz) wholemeal flour
75 g (3 oz) white flour
75 g (3 oz) margarine
3-5 tablespoons cold water

Tin: Sandwich tin 23 cm (9") diameter.

Mix the flours together and rub in the margarine until like fine breadcrumbs. (A food processor will do this in seconds.) Add just enough water to bind together. Squeeze pastry together. Turn out onto a floured surface and roll out and use to line the tin.

Filling:
1 onion, chopped
25 g (1 oz) margarine
1-2 cloves garlic
110 g (4 oz) mushrooms, sliced
225 g (8 oz) smoked mackerel fillets
Juice ½ lemon
2 large eggs
Mug milk (225 ml/8 fl oz) (see note)
2 tablespoons mayonnaise
1 teaspoon mustard
Salt and freshly ground black pepper

Note: Very occasionally yield to temptation and use cream instead of milk!

Cooking Time: About 45 minutes (200°C, 400°F, Gas 6)

Lightly fry the onion in the margarine until soft then add the garlic and mushrooms and fry until soft also. Spread out (juices and all) over the base of the pastry case. Remove any skin from the smoked mackerel, breaking the fillets into bite sized chunks and scatter them over the mushroom mixture. Sprinkle the lemon juice over everything.

Whisk together the eggs, milk, mayonnaise and mustard. Season with minimum salt (because of the fish) and pepper, and pour into the pastry case to just cover the contents. Bake until well cooked and golden brown. Even though the top may look cooked, don't cut down on the cooking time, to ensure that the pastry is thoroughly cooked. There is nothing worse than soggy pastry at the bottom of a quiche! I find the brown shortcrust pastry is particularly good at giving a nice crisp pastry case.

Smoked Salmon Quiche (F)

(Serves 5-8)

Ideal for special occasions. Excellent also to serve as a starter (hot) cut in narrow wedges decorated with a little lettuce, tomato and lemon wedge.

Instead of the smoked mackerel, use slices of **smoked salmon (150-175 g/5-6 oz).** Don't chop it, simply lay the slices all over the mushroom and onion mixture in the pastry case. Sprinkle with the lemon juice and pour in the egg mixture to just barely cover. When baked the smoked salmon will show through and look most luxurious.

Mushroom Quiche (F)

(Serves 5-6)

Use the Smoked Mackerel Quiche recipe. Omit the smoked mackerel altogether. Increase the amount of **mushrooms to 450 g(1 lb)** Also add **¼-½ teaspoon nutmeg.** (Don't omit the lemon juice). Scatter **50 g (2 oz) grated cheese** over the top of the quiche half way through the cooking time.

Spinach Quiche (F)

(Serves 5-6)

Use the Smoked Mackerel Quiche recipe. Omit the smoked mackerel and use **450 g (1 lb) fresh spinach**, cooked and chopped. Omit the lemon juice and use ½ **level teaspoon of nutmeg**. Scatter **50 g (2 oz) grated cheese** over the top of the quiche half way through the cooking time.

To cook spinach: first rinse in plenty of water, don't shake off the excess water. Cook in a saucepan with no added water, and the lid on. The volume of the spinach will reduce greatly.

Hot Tomatoes Stuffed with Tuna

(Serves 4)

Ideal as a starter or light meal dish

4 beef tomatoes or 8 tomatoes
50 g (2 oz) margarine or butter
1 small onion, finely chopped
1-2 cloves garlic, crushed
110 g (4 oz) wholemeal breadcrumbs
100 g (3½ oz) tin tuna steak (or salmon), drained
1 stick celery , finely chopped
Salt and freshly ground black pepepr
¼ teaspoon mixed herbs
1 large egg, beaten
Juice ½-1 orange

Cooking Time: Bake for 15-25 minutes (190°C, 375°F, Gas 5).

Cut a lid off each tomato — opposite end to the stalk. Scoop out fleshy insides. Fry the onion and garlic in the margarine until soft. Add in all the other ingredients using the egg and the orange juice to moisten. Mix well.

Spoon into the tomatoes.

Stand tomatoes, in a greased ovenproof dish, and cook until tomatoes soften somewhat and heat to piping hot.

Accompany with a green salad if serving as a meal.

Use up the fleshy insides in a soup.

MEATS

(Q) = quick to cook   (F) = suitable for freezing

Lean meat is a very nutritious food, it is also high in iron. At the same time, it is better not to eat great quantities of it. For this reason I love to bulk out my meat recipes whenever possible with vegetables and stuffings. This has the added advantage of extra flavour and economy. Try my delicious Meatloaf recipe, the mushrooms and breadcrumbs add flavour and bulk. The same mixture can be used to make really tasty hamburgers.

The actual process of mincing meat creates a certain amount of heat, which warms up the meat. This moist warmth in a protein rich food is an ideal environment for dangerous bacteria to develop. Therefore it is important to cook minced meat on the day of purchase. However, cooking at high temperatures kills harmful bacteria.

Stuffing Topped Chops

(Serves 4)

Stuffing not only adds 'bulk' to food, it also adds great flavour. This is a really handy way to use it - just pile it on top of the chops and bake - delicious!

4 lamp chops - gigot (see note 1)
75 g (3 oz) margarine
1 medium onion, finely chopped
1-2 cloves garlic, crushed or chopped
1-2 sticks celery, finely chopped
75 g (3 oz) approx. breadcrumbs - preferably wholemeal
Salt and freshly ground black pepper
1 teaspoon chopped fresh rosemary
OR 1 teaspoon mixed herbs (see note 2)
1 tablespoon chopped parsley
Juice 1 orange

Cooking Time: About 1-1½ hours (190°C, 375°F, Gas 5). Reduce heat after 45 minutes to (180°C, 350°F, Gas 4).

Note 1: Choose chops that have had the bones removed. They will be a bit "stringy", use wooden cocktail sticks to 'skewer' them into a neat shape. Cut away excess fat.

Note 2: Dried rosemary can be very spikey so it is not a suitable substitute in this recipe.

First fry the chops in a pan using 50 g (2 oz) of the margarine just to brown them a little on each side. Transfer them to a tin. Add the remaining 25 g (1 oz) margarine to the same pan (unless you have sufficient fat left in the pan). Add the onion and fry until soft, then add in the garlic. Next add the celery, breadcrumbs, pepper and salt, also the rosemary and parsley. Moisten with orange juice.

Place spoonfuls of this stuffing mixture on top of the chops. Press the stuffing down to cover the whole top of the chops and to steady it in place. Pour a little bit of water (about 4-6 tablespoons) into the tin. Cover the chops well with foil - but don't close it tightly.

Cook until chops are nicely tender. Remove the foil for the last 10 minutes to crisp the top of the stuffing. Remove cocktail sticks before serving.

Braised Chops

(Serves 4-5)

The chops are cooked on a bed of vegetables and each flavours the other deliciously! A meal-in-a-dish.

1 onion, chopped
50 g (2 oz) margarine
1-2 cloves garlic, crushed or chopped
2 potatoes, peeled and diced
2 sticks celery, chopped
2 carrots, diced
1 leek, thinly sliced
Salt and freshly ground black pepper
Sprig of fresh thyme and fresh rosemary
OR 1 level teaspoon mixed herbs
½ chicken stock cube
275 ml (½ pint) boiling water
4-6 lamb chops (gigot)

To serve:
Chopped fresh parsley

Dish: Ovenproof dish, wide enough for chops to sit side by side.

Cooking Time: About 1¼-1½ hours (190°C, 375°F, Gas 5). After about 40 minutes reduce heat (180°C, 350°F, Gas 4).

Note: Choose chops with bones removed. This will make them sort of broken up and 'stringy' in appearance. Use wooden cocktail sticks to hold each one together in a neat shape.

Lightly fry the onion in 25 g (1 oz) of the margarine to soften it and add the garlic. Put the other prepared vegetables into a bowl and add the onion and garlic to them along with the salt, pepper and the herbs. Dissolve the stock cube in the water. Place the vegetable mixture in the ovenproof dish and pour in the stock.

Cut any excess fat off the chops. Lightly fry them in the remaining margarine just to brown them on either side. Sit chops on top of the layer of vegetables. Cover dish with a well fitting lid - or with foil, well wrapped around (to prevent stock drying out). Bake until the chops are tender. Remove foil towards the end of the cooking time to sort of crisp the chops. Remove any cocktail sticks.

Serve chops with the juicy vegetables, which will be a little overcooked but their flavour is delicious! Sprinkle liberally with chopped fresh parsley. Accompany with crusty bread or potatoes.

Lamb, Carrot and Orange Casserole (F)

(Serves 5-6)

The name tells it all. The flavour is excellent. The orange and celery give a 'lightness' which is great because lamb can have quite a 'heavy' flavour.

1 large onion, chopped
25 g (1 oz) margarine
2 cloves garlic, crushed or chopped
450-550 g (1-1¼ lbs) lean stewing lamb pieces
450 g (1 lb) carrots, scraped and sliced
225 g (8 oz) celery (about 3 sticks) chopped
Juice of 2 oranges (150 ml/¼ pt)
900 ml (1½ pts) water
1 chicken stock cube (see note)
1 teaspoon mixed herbs
1 teaspoon dried rosemary
OR small sprig fresh rosemary
Salt and freshly ground black pepper
1 generous teaspoon honey
1 rounded teaspoon mustard (grainy)
2 heaped teaspoons cornflour
2 tablespoons chopped fresh parsley

Note: If fresh chicken stock is available, it can be used instead of the stock cube and water. If cooking in a casserole in the oven, it speeds up the cooking time to use boiling water or stock.

Cooking Time: On top of cooker - about 1 hour OR
In oven - about 1½ hours (180°C, 350°F, Gas 4)

Fry the onion in the margarine in a frying pan until soft. Add the garlic. Transfer to a saucepan (heavy bottomed). Next fry the lamb pieces to brown lightly. Add to the onion. Add all the remaining ingredients to the onion and meat EXCEPT the cornflour and parsley. Bring to the boil, simmer gently with lid on until meat is tender.

Blend the cornflour with a little water and add to the saucepan. Bring to the boil, stirring, to thicken. Serve scattered generously with parsley.

This dish can also be cooked in a casserole in the oven. Simply put all the ingredients into a casserole instead of the saucepan and cook in the oven until meat is tender. Pour the juices off, thicken them in a saucepan with the cornflour, add the parsley and return to the casserole.

Chunky Pork and Tomato Dish - (A Sort of Stir-Fry) (Q)

(Serves 4-5)

Although this dish is cooked like a stir-fry, the addition of a tin of tomatoes gives it a lovely 'cooked in a casserole' quality.

1 pork steak, about 350-450 g (¾-1 lb)
2-3 tablespoons oil
1 onion, thinly sliced
1-2 cloves garlic, crushed
150 g (5 oz) mushrooms, sliced
225 g (8 oz) courgettes, neatly chopped
Salt and freshly ground black pepper
½ level teaspoon herbes de Provence (or mixed herbs)
¼-½ teaspoon cayenne pepper
2 teaspoons sugar
1-2 tablespoons soy sauce
1 rounded teaspoon cornflour
1 tin chopped tomatoes

To serve:
Boiled rice or crusty bread
Natural yogurt (optional)

Slice the pork steak into thin slices (about 1 cm/½" thick). Cut away any membrane (shiny skin), or fat. Prepare all the vegetables.

Heat the oil in a wok (or frying pan) and fry the pieces of pork, 5-6 at a time, until a nice golden brown on each side. (See note at end). Lift out the cooked pieces and keep to one side. Next fry the onion until soft, then add in the garlic, mushrooms and courgettes. Season with salt, pepper, herbs, cayenne pepper, sugar and soy sauce. Toss everything together as it cooks for about 5 minutes.

Blend the cornflour with a little cold water and add to the vegetables along with the tin of chopped tomatoes. Also add in the fried pork. Bring to the boil, stirring everything together. Simmer for a few minutes and serve.

Accompany with natural or Greek style yogurt, served in a bowl, spoon a little on top of each serving.

Note: If too many pork pieces are put on the pan together, they produce moisture and so they are 'steamed' rather than fried.

Chunky Chicken and Tomato Dish (Q)

(Serves 4-5)

Use **350-450 g (¾-1 lb) boneless chicken breast fillets** instead of the pork in the above recipe.

Sweet Barbecue Sauce with Spare Ribs

(Serves 4-6)

Finger licking stuff! This delicious sauce can be baked on spare ribs in the oven or used as a dip for barbecued spare ribs and other meats.

Sauce:
3 tablespoons tomato ketchup
3 tablespoons honey
3 tablespoons brown sugar (demerara)
1 teaspoon mustard (grainy)
½ level teaspoon cayenne pepper (hot!)
1 tablespoon vinegar
2 tablespoons soy sauce
Salt and freshly ground black pepper

1.125-1.4 kg (2½-3 lbs) spare ribs (see note).
Salt and freshly ground black pepper

Cooking Time: Pre-cook for about 45-60 minutes without sauce (180°C, 350°F, Gas 4) until tender. Then add the sauce and cook for an extra 20-30 minutes OR brown pre-cooked ribs on barbecue and serve with the sauce.

Note: Spare ribs come in different shapes and sizes depending on your butcher. Some sell slices of belly of pork, which are nice and meaty, also nice and fatty! Allow 1-4 per person (about 350 g/12 oz each). Another type are the 'sheets' of boney ribs with very little meat and almost no fat on them. Allow about 350 g (12 oz) per person. Remove the layer of "white" shiny membrane from the back of the ribs as it is really tough! Use a sharp knife to loosen it a bit, then use your fingers and pull really firmly - it pulls right off.

To make the sauce: Delicious! Simply mix all the ingredients together! This can be made in advance and kept in a covered jar.

To cook spare ribs:

Pre-cook: Place sheets of ribs (round side upwards) or individual ribs in a foil lined tin. Season with salt and pepper and cover well with more foil (to keep in any moisture). Pre-cook in oven until meat is tender. It will not appear or smell very attractive at this stage!

To finish in oven: Fold back the foil, spoon any excess fat (not juice) off the tin. Cut the 'sheets' into separate ribs and return to tin, round side downwards. Spoon the sauce mixture generously all over the ribs and return to the oven (uncovered). Cook until ribs brown and are flavoured by the sauce - delicious. Be careful not to cook too long or the sauce will burn.

To finish on barbecue: Lift ribs out of tin. Cut 'sheets' into separate ribs. Place over hot barbecue to brown deliciously, brush with oil if necessary. Serve the ribs with the sauce as a dip, or spooned over them on a plate. The dip cannot be brushed on the meat as it barbecues because of its high sugar content it will burn dreadfully.

Serve with paper towels or damp towels!

Coleslaw and baked potatoes go well with this dish.

Chicken Joints in Sweet Barbecue Sauce

(Serves 4-5)

Use enough **chicken joints (with bones in)** to serve 4-5 persons. Use instead of spare ribs in the above recipe.

Extra Virgin Olive Oil on the label means that the olives have just been washed and pressed to squeeze out the oil. If necessary the oil is filtered and then bottled. No other treatment is given. The flavour of this oil is directly related to the olives used (just like wine and grapes). **Fine Virgin Olive Oil** is the same except it has a slightly higher acid content. **Olive Oil** on the label denotes oil made from the second and third pressings of the olive, which includes various treatments and blendings. This is perfectly adequate to use, though not as flavoursome and also not as expensive!

Pork and Vegetable Curried Casserole (F)

(Serves 5-6)

The hint of sweetness given by the raisins and chutney combines very well with the pork and vegetables. This is a very tasty casserole, with lots of vegetables - not heavy but light in flavour.

700 g (1½ lbs) lean pork pieces
75 g (3 oz) margarine
2 onions, thinly sliced
2-4 heaped teaspoons curry powder
1 tablespoon flour
450 g (1 lb) carrots, sliced
2 sticks celery, chopped
1 tin chopped tomatoes
900 ml (1½ pts) water
1 chicken stock cube (OR fresh chicken stock)
50 g (2 oz) raisins (or sultanas)
1 tablespoon tomato purée
1-2 tablespoons chutney
½ cooking apple, peeled and chopped
Salt and freshly ground black pepper

Cooking Time: On top of cooker - about 1 hour OR
In oven for about 1½-2 hours (180°C, 350°F, Gas 4), (use boiling water or stock to speed up oven cooking).

Fry the pork pieces (in two or three lots) in 50 g (2 oz) of the margarine until nicely browned. Transfer to a saucepan (the heavier the better) or into a casserole. The remaining fat in the pan will probably contain overcooked scrappy bits - I usually completely wipe out the pan with a paper towel and then melt the remaining 25 g (1 oz) margarine. In this, fry the onions until soft and add in the curry powder (2 teaspoons will give a very light curry flavour, for a more positive flavour I use 4 teaspoons). Fry for a minute or two, then transfer to the saucepan (or casserole) along with all the remaining ingredients. Bring the saucepan to the boil, cover with a lid and simmer gently until meat is tender. (If using casserole, cover with lid and cook in oven until meat is tender).

Serve with boiled rice or potatoes.

Roast Stuffed Loin of Pork

(Serves 6-8)

This is very tasty indeed and excellent for a special occasion. I prefer not to roll up this joint - but to leave it flat. When cooked, it can be carved just like slicing bread!

1.5-1.8 kg (3½-4 lbs) centre loin roast (see note)

Stuffing:
1 small onion
50 g (2 oz) margarine
1 clove garlic
1½ mugs (110 g/4 oz) wholemeal breadcrumbs
½ medium cooking apple, finely chopped
1-2 sticks celery, finely chopped
Finely grated rind of ½ lemon
Salt and freshly ground black pepper
1 level teaspoon herbes de Provence (or mixed herbs)
1 tablespoon chopped fresh parsley
¼ teaspoon nutmeg
Juice of 1 orange
Wooden cocktail sticks

To finish:
2-4 teaspoons mustard (a nice grainy one)
110 g (4 oz) approx. brown sugar (demerara)

Note: Ask the butcher to cut out the bones from the pork and to remove the skin, leaving a layer of fat (not too thick). Also ask for a "pocket" for stuffing the full length of the joint. Ask him not to roll the joint but to leave it flat.

Cooking Time: Roast meat, allowing about 25 minutes for every 450 g (1 lb) of meat plus an extra 45 minutes at the end (190°C, 375°F, Gas 5). Plan for meat to be ready ½ hour before the meal, to allow it time to 'relax' and thus make it easier to carve.

Make the stuffing:
Fry the chopped onion in the margarine until soft and add the garlic and fry. Add the contents of the pan to the breadcrumbs in a bowl. Add the finely chopped apple and celery. Stir in the lemon rind, salt and pepper, herbs, fresh parsley and nutmeg. Mix everything together and moisten with the orange juice.

Fill the pocket with the stuffing. Pin closed with cocktail sticks. Place joint flat on a foil lined roasting tin with the fat side upwards. Close foil over meat and place in oven. Cook until just tender.

A good half an hour before the end of cooking time, fold back the foil, pour off any juices, spread the mustard all over the fat and then spread the brown sugar thickly on top.

Return to oven, raise heat (200°C, 400°F, Gas 6). Cook until sugar melts and the fat looks nice and crusty.

Take out of oven and allow to stand in a warm place for about 20 minutes before carving in neat slices.

Pork Stir-Fry with Apple Juice (Q)

(Serves 4-6)

This recipe makes the most of a small pork steak. The choice of vegetables is what I call 'Irish' and they combine excellently.

1 medium carrot
150 g (5 oz) cauliflower
2 sticks celery
75 g (3 oz) green beans, frozen or fresh
1 onion
1 clove garlic
1 pork steak

Sauce mix:
150 ml (¼ pt) apple juice
2-3 tablespoons soy sauce
Salt and freshly ground black pepper
1 heaped teaspoon cornflour
1 teaspoon sugar

To fry:
About 4 tablespoons oil

First prepare the ingredients. Cut the carrots into 5 cm (2") lengths and then cut these up into thin "sticks". This is to ensure quick cooking. Break the cauliflower into small little florets. Cut the celery into sticks to match the carrot, also cut the green beans into 5 cm (2") lengths. Thinly slice the onion and crush or chop the garlic. Cut the pork steak into thin slices, removing any membrane or fat. If the slices are large compared to the prepared vegetables, cut them in half or in strips.

Mix together the sauce ingredients in a separate bowl. Heat the oil in a wok (or use a large frying pan or saucepan). Add the pork (in two or three lots) and fry until golden brown and cooked through. Lift out cooked pieces and keep to one side.

Wipe out the wok or pan and add fresh oil. Now add carrots and cauliflower and fry, tossing in the oil for a few minutes. Then add the celery, green beans, onion and garlic and continue frying and tossing for another few minutes to cook vegetables a little more. Next add the pork back into the wok with the vegetables. Also pour in the sauce mixture. Bring to the boil, stirring and tossing, then simmer for a few minutes until vegetables are bite tender.

Serve with rice or noodles (try Chinese Egg Noodles).

Chicken Stir-Fry with Apple Juice (Q)

(Serves 4-5)

Skinless chicken breast fillets (3 of them) can be used instead of pork steak in the above recipe. Cut the chicken breasts into thin fingers.

Stir-frys do not reheat well because they lose their crispness which is part of their attraction.

Diets too high in saturated fats lead to a build up of too much cholesterol in the blood stream which can cling to the lining of the blood vessels thus making them narrower and easier to block. The only way of knowing if your blood contains too much cholesterol is to have it tested.

Pot Roast of Beef (F)

(Serves 6-8)

Pot roasting may have old fashioned connotations - but this method of cooking is ideal for the leaner more health conscious roasts we have today (as well as the less tender ones). Cooked in a heavy pot or casserole with some stock and vegetables the meat is deliciously flavoured, juicy and tender! Traditionally done on the cooler corner of the range, pot roasting nowadays is usually done in the oven.

1.4-1.8 kg (3-4 lb) joint beef (see note)
25 g (1 oz) margarine or 2 tablespoons oil
1 onion, sliced
2 cloves garlic, chopped
1 beef stock cube dissolved in 275 ml
(½ pt) boiling water
Salt and freshly ground black pepper
1 level teaspoon mixed herbs
OR 1 fresh bay leaf and 1 sprig fresh parsley
1 heaped teaspoon gravy powder
1 heaped teaspoon soup powder
(from a packet of beef or oxtail soup)

Note: Joints of beef which are suitable.
       Very lean - topside, silverside, round roast
       Less tender - housekeeper's cut, brisket, these can be quite fatty, so choose the leanest.

Variation: 150 ml (¼ pt) of boiling water can be omitted and 150 ml (¼ pt) of red wine can be added instead to the dissolved stock.

Cooking Time: About 2½-3 hours (170°C, 325°F, Gas 3)

The first thing to do is to fry the joint of beef to brown it all over in the margarine. This can be done in the cooking pot/casserole but I prefer to do this in a frying pan. Then transfer the meat to the pot or casserole.

Next fry the onion until just golden and add the garlic and put with the meat. Pour in the dissolved stock. Season lightly with salt and pepper and add the herbs. Cover the pot or casserole with a well fitting lid. Place in the oven and cook until tender.

50

Lift out the meat and keep it warm. Pour the cooking juices into a jug and leave to stand for a few minutes so that the fat rises to the surface and you can spoon it off (a few ice cubes added helps to "set" the fat quickly). Blend the gravy powder and the soup powder with a little water. Add to the juices and bring to the boil in a saucepan and serve with the meat.

Serve with vegetables of your choice.

Reheating: This dish can be cooked in advance because the slices of meat can be put into the gravy and reheated when required. Servings of meat can be frozen in the gravy.

Pot Roast of Pork (F)

A **joint of fillet (leg) of pork** (about the same weight as the beef), though very lean, can be quite dry. Cooked as a pot roast, it is lovely and moist. Use a **chicken stock cube** instead of beef. This will cook in a shorter time (about 2-2½ hours). Omit the gravy and soup powder, instead use **2 level teaspoons cornflour** to thicken the juices. Servings of meat can be frozen in the gravy.

Butter and margarine have much the same amount of calories - what differs is the type of fat that they are.

Orange juice not only gives a nice sharp, sweet taste to recipes, but also includes Vitamin C (ascorbic acid) which helps the body to absorb iron from the diet more effectively.

Chilli Con Carne (F)

(Serves 5-6)

When you see the list of ingredients for this recipe, you may be tempted to run for a packet of mix - but hopefully you won't because this is delicious. The ingredients are very simple - just a little bit of this and a little bit of that. The inclusion of cocoa is inspired by traditional Mexican cooking.

2 medium sized onions (about 75 g/3 oz)
2 tablespoons oil
2-3 cloves garlic, crushed or chopped
450 g (1 lb) lean minced beef
2-3 level teaspoons chilli powder
1-2 level teaspoons ground cumin (optional)
1 level teaspoon oregano (or mixed herbs)
1 heaped teaspoon cocoa powder
1 tin chopped tomatoes (400 g/14 oz)
2 teaspoons tomato purée
150 ml (¼ pt) water
1 beef stock cube
1 tablespoon chutney
50 g (2 oz) raisins or sultanas
1 tin red kidney beans (425 g/15 oz), drained
1 small green pepper (110 g/4 oz) (optional)
1 small yellow pepper (110 g/4 oz) (optional)
Salt and freshly ground black pepper

Fry the onions in the oil until soft and add in the garlic. Next add in minced meat (in two lots) and fry, breaking up the lumps, until well browned all over. Tilt pan to one side to allow the excess fat (if any) to run down, spoon it off. Transfer the meat to a saucepan.

To the saucepan add all the remaining ingredients. Do note that the chilli powder is very hot so don't be generous with it unless your family want it that way! The cumin is optional - it has what I call a Mexican flavour. The quantity can be increased if you like it. The cocoa gives a subtle flavour and colour to the dish. Initially I used to use only half of the tin of kidney beans (freezing the other half) then as my family got to like them, I increased the amount.

Bring the saucepan to the boil, stirring frequently. Cover with a lid and simmer very gently for about 30-40 minutes. Serve with rice, potatoes or tacos (Mexican pancakes).

This is a great dish to make in advance and reheat.

Beefy Pancake Pile-Up (F)

(Serves 6)

The pancakes are stacked with meat sauce spread between them. A real family favourite. Can be made in advance.

Meat sauce:
1 onion, chopped
2-3 tablespoons oil
2-3 cloves garlic, crushed
550 g (1¼ lb) minced lean beef
1 tin chopped tomatoes
1-2 tablespoons tomato purée
Salt and freshly ground black pepper
1 level teaspoon mustard
½-1 level teaspoon oregano
¼ level teaspoon nutmeg
1 rounded tablespoon soup powder (from a packet of beef or oxtail soup)
1 mug cold water (250 ml/8 fl oz)

Pancakes: (10 pancakes, about 23 cm (9") diameter)
175 g (6 oz) flour
75 g (3 oz) wholemeal flour (see note)
2 large eggs
570 ml (1 pt) milk
2 teaspoons oil
1 tablespoon chopped fresh chives or parsley (optional)

Note: If preferred, omit the wholemeal and use all white flour.

Cooking Time: No need to cook if everything is hot. However, a little baking 'sets' it nicely together - about 25 minutes (190°C, 375°F, Gas 5).

If made up in advance and cooking from cold, allow an extra 20 minutes at reduced heat (180°C, 350°F, Gas 4).

To make meat sauce:
The meat sauce needs to be fairly runny. Fry the chopped onion until soft in the oil and add in the garlic. Then add in the minced beef (in two lots) and fry, breaking up the lumps, until nicely browned all over. Tilt the pan to allow any excess fat run down, spoon it off. (If your pan is small, transfer the browned meat to a saucepan.)

Add in all the remaining ingredients. Stir well, bring to the boil and then simmer gently for about 20 minutes.

To make pancakes:
Put all the ingredients into a bowl (except half the milk). Whisk gently, then briskly to make a smooth batter or buzz in a food processor. Add in the remaining milk. Leave batter to stand for 20-30 minutes before frying to allow the flour absorb the liquid.

Fry in a hot greased pan using nearly ¾ ladleful for each pancake. When golden underneath, turn over (as I lift I give a quick rub to the pan with a lump of margarine to grease it lightly). Fry until golden and cooked. Pancakes can be stored in a pile until required.

To assemble: Spread the meat sauce between the layers of pancakes. If baking in the oven, cover completely with foil.

Moussaka (F)

(Serves 5-6)

This dish is often called the Shepherd's pie of the Balkans! As with any classic recipe, there are many variations. This one is usually associated with Greece. The meat sauce is alternated with layers of sliced aubergines. You can give it an Irish 'twist' and use potatoes instead. The dish is topped with a yogurt mixture which browns delightfully when cooked.

1 large onion, chopped
2 tablespoons oil, preferably olive oil
2-4 cloves garlic, crushed or chopped
450 g (1 lb) minced lamb or beef (see note)
2 tablespoons flour
275 ml (½ pt) beef stock (use a cube if necessary)
1 tablespoon tomato purée
4 tomatoes, chopped
50-110 g (2-4 oz) mushrooms, chopped
Salt and freshly ground black pepper
¼ teaspoon nutmeg
A sprig of fresh rosemary OR 1 level teaspoon dried rosemary
2-3 large aubergines, unpeeled OR 4-6 large potatoes - (cooked)
Oil for frying (preferably olive oil)

Topping:
175 ml (6 fl oz) milk
2 rounded teaspoons cornflour
1 carton (125 ml) natural yogurt
1 large egg
Salt and freshly ground black pepper
75 g (3 oz) grated cheese (optional)

Cooking Time: Cook for about 45 minutes (190°C, 375°F, Gas 5), reduce heat if necessary.

Note: Minced lamb has a flavour of its own and is worth trying occasionally. Left over roast lamb, minced, can also be used, though flavour will be a bit different. No need to fry this at the start of preparation.

Meat Sauce:
Fry the onion in the oil until soft, then add in the garlic. Next add the minced meat in two lots and fry, breaking up the lumps, until it is browned well all over. Add in the flour, mix through and then stir in the stock and tomato purée. Now add in the tomatoes and mushrooms. Season with salt and pepper and flavour with nutmeg and sprig of rosemary.

Bring to the boil and then turn off the heat. Leave to stand with lid on to hold in the heat while preparing the aubergines (or potatoes). Discard sprig of rosemary just before assembling the dish.

To prepare the aubergines (or potatoes):
Slice the unpeeled aubergines, discarding the stalks (see note, page 66). You will need enough slices to make three layers. Fry the slices in oil to brown them. (The aubergines soak up oil!) Prepare the peeled potatoes in the same way. (It is necessary to use cooked potatoes because the moussaka is not long enough in the oven to cook them.)

To prepare the topping:
Blend the milk into the cornflour and bring to the boil to thicken. Cool somewhat and mix in the yogurt, egg and seasoning.

To assemble:
Line the bottom of an ovenproof dish with aubergine (or potato) slices. Cover with half the meat sauce. Place a second layer of aubergine slices on top and cover with the remaining meat sauce. Put final layer of aubergine slices on top and cover with topping (see note).

Bake uncovered until top turns a lovely golden brown and dish is piping hot.

Serve with salad and crusty bread.

Note: If preparing in advance, don't put topping on until ready to cook, otherwise it might sink down through the meat mixture.

Meatloaf (F)

The fried mushrooms help to give a wonderful flavour to my version of this American classic recipe. This makes a great substitute for a roast, with lots of cutting. Eat hot with gravy or cold with salad.

50 g (2 oz) margarine or 45 ml (3 tablespoons) oil
1 medium - large onion, finely chopped
225 g (8 oz) mushrooms, chopped
2-3 cloves garlic, crushed or chopped
700 g (1½ lb) minced lean beef (rib or round)
225 g (8 oz) minced lean pork (or sausage meat) (see note)
110 g (4 oz) wholemeal breadcrumbs
1 tablespoon flour
Salt and freshly ground black pepper
½ level teaspoon nutmeg
1 level teaspoon mixed herbs
1 generous tablespoon chopped parsley
1-2 tablespoons soy sauce or Worcester sauce
1-2 tablespoons tomato ketchup
2 large eggs

Note: Buy pork pieces and "buzz" them in food processor to mince. Can be omitted if you wish.

Tin: Loaf tin, 23 cm x 12.5 cm x 7.5 cm (9" x 5" x 3" deep) greased (a piece of greaseproof or foil in the base helps turn out meatloaf easily). The meatloaf can be shaped into a rectangle and baked on a flat tin.

Cooking Time: About 1¼-1½ hours (190°C, 375°F, Gas 5). After 45 minutes, reduce heat (180°C, 350°F, Gas 4) if the meatloaf is browning nicely.

Heat the margarine or oil in a frying pan and fry the onion until soft. Add in the mushrooms and fry until soft, slightly golden and reduced in volume. Add the garlic and fry.

Put the meats, breadcrumbs, flour, seasoning, spice and herbs into a bowl. Add in the soy sauce, tomato ketchup and the eggs. Pour the onion and mushroom mixture (including all juices) into the bowl.

Now mix everything together. (I find it easiest to use my hands, with disposable gloves, because I can really squeeze everything together.) Turn into the tin and smooth top. **Or** shape into a rectangle about 7.5 cm/3" deep, and place on a greased tin.

Bake until cooked through. When top gets nicely browned, cover with foil. Serve hot or cold with gravy.

(Chicken fat from roasting chicken used instead of margarine adds even more flavour).

Variation: Reduce the meat by 225 g (8 oz) and add an extra 110 g (4 oz) each mushrooms and breadcrumbs. Brush top with oil before cooking.

Deluxe Hamburgers (Q) (F)

If you want to make the most delicious hamburgers you have ever made - use the Meatloaf mixture (omit the pork) and instead of putting it into a tin, shape into hamburgers (about 8-10) and fry or grill gently until cooked through (about 5-8 minutes each side). Try to avoid making the hamburgers too thick as they take too long to cook.

Serve with the gravy or in burger buns.

Gravy (Q)

If there are any juices left from the meat with which you plan to serve gravy, save them, removing any fat.

1 small onion, chopped
25 g (1 oz) margarine
1 clove garlic, crushed
50 g (2 oz) mushrooms, chopped
15 g (½ oz) flour
275–425 ml (½ – ¾ pt) water
½ chicken or beef stock cube
Juices of meat with which the gravy is being served
1 small glass of dry/medium sherry or red wine (optional)
2 tablespoons of oyster sauce (from a bottle)

Fry the onion in the margarine until soft and add in the mushrooms and garlic. Fry until soft. Stir in the flour over the heat. Add in the water and stock cube and stir briskly (using a wire whisk). Add meat juices, sherry and oyster sauce. Bring to the boil, stirring briskly. (If sherry or wine has been used, boil briskly for 1-2 minutes.) Simmer for a few minutes. Serve.

Apple Juice Sauce (Q)

(Serves 4-6)

This tasty sauce with its sharp/sweet flavour is really good with ham, bacon or pork, also with fish and chicken.

1 large onion, chopped
25 g (1 oz) margarine
1-2 cloves garlic, crushed or chopped
1 medium cooking apple (175 g/6 oz) chopped finely
1-2 sticks celery, chopped finely
425-570 ml (¾-1 pt) apple juice
Salt and freshly ground black pepper
1 teaspoon sugar
1 level teaspoon mixed herbs (or sage)
3 rounded teaspoons cornflour
2 tablespoons chopped fresh, parsley or chives

Use a saucepan or a deepish frying pan. Fry the onion in the margarine until it is soft and add in the garlic. Next add in the apple and celery and cook for a minute or two. Then add in the apple juice, salt, pepper, sugar and mixed herbs. Bring to the boil and then simmer gently with the lid on for about 3-5 minutes until all is soft.

Blend the cornflour with a little water and add to the sauce. Bring to boil, stirring, to thicken. Buzz sauce in a food processor, then reheat, OR better still, serve as it is, a nice chunky sauce. Stir in the parsley.

Note: Instead of apple juice use a dry cider to make the above sauce.

Ham (or Bacon) with Apple Juice Sauce (Q)

Slices of home cooked ham or bacon are added to the sauce and heated through. This not only tastes delicious but also the meat keeps its lovely pink colour. Use about **700g (1½ lb) home cooked ham or bacon.** Slice the meat, add to **Apple Juice Sauce,** bring to boil, simmer for a few minutes and turn into a serving dish. Scatter with chopped parsley.

Pork Chops in Apple Juice Sauce

Brown the **4-6 lean pork chops** on both sides in **some margarine** in a frying pan. Transfer to an ovenproof dish, laying chops side by side. Pour **Apple Juice Sauce** over them. Cover dish tightly with foil and bake for 1½-1¾ hours until chops are succulently tender. (180°C, 350°F, Gas 4).

OR

Add browned chops to the Apple Juice Sauce in a wide based saucepan so chops can sit in a single layer. Bring to boil, cover with lid and simmer very gently until chops are very tender Don't allow them to burn!

Mackerel in Apple Juice Sauce (Q)

Place **fillets of mackerel (approx 4-6)** in an ovenproof dish, cover with the hot **Apple Juice Sauce** and bake for 20-30 minutes (190°C, 375°F, Gas 5).

Bacon Loaf

(Serves 6)

This bacon loaf is equally delicious eaten hot or cold. The grated apple gives a delightful hint of sharp sweetness to the mixture. Cooked ham, or a mixture of cooked turkey and ham can be used instead of the bacon - handy at Christmas!

450 g (1 lb) lean cooked bacon
1 large onion, finely chopped
50 g (2 oz) margarine or 4 tablespoons oil
2 cloves garlic, crushed or chopped
1 stick of celery, finely chopped
1 large cooking apple, grated
50 g (2 oz) porridge meal
50 g (2 oz) flour
Freshly ground black pepper
A little salt
½ teaspoon mustard
¼ teaspoon nutmeg
2 tablespoons chopped parsley
2 large eggs
4 tablespoons stock or milk

Tin: Loaf tin - 23 cm x 12.5 cm x 7.5 cm deep (9" x 5" x 3" deep) greased. Line the bottom with foil or baking parchment.

Cooking Time: About 1 hour (190°C, 375°F, Gas 5), reduce heat after about 40 minutes (180°C, 350°F, Gas 4) if it is browning nicely.

Mince the bacon by 'buzzing' in food processor or put through a mincer or else chop very finely. Put into a bowl.

Fry the onion in the margarine until soft then add in the garlic and fry. Then put contents of the pan into the bowl together with all the remaining ingredients. Mix very well together. (I use my hands with disposable gloves, it is very quick and effective).

Put the mixture into the prepared tin, smooth out, cover with foil and bake until nicely set and cooked through. Loosen sides from tin and turn out.

Serve hot with parsley sauce or with Apple Juice Sauce. Serve cold with mayonnaise.

Variation: Include 110 g (4 oz) wholemeal breadcrumbs in the mixture, increase the stock or milk by 2-3 tablespoons. Brush top with melted margarine before cooking.

Chicken stir-fry with pineapple

Smoked trout cheesecake

Carrot and pineapple cake

Beefy pancake pile-up and Lamb, carrot and orange casserole

Vegetable and smoked fish soup

Stuffing topped cod

Anti-clockwise: Caponata,
Carrots in orange juice,
Nutty cauliflower purée

Chocolate yogurt cake

Brandy snaps

VEGETABLES

(Q) = quick to cook   (F) = suitable for freezing

I love vegetables! The range of fresh vegetables available to us all the year round is marvellous. Many surveys show that the Mediterranean diet (which is rich in vegetables, fruit and olive oil) is particularly healthy for the heart. Vegetables are rich in vitamins and some minerals and are mostly low in fat and high in fibre.

Some of the recipes I include are suitable as a main dish such as the tasty Mushroom and Nut Loaf or the Vegetable Lasagne. Other recipes are more suitable as an accompaniment - such as my delicious Nutty Cauliflower Purée or the Caponata with its sweet/sour flavour.

The Bulgar, Rice and Pasta Dishes are not strictly vegetable dishes, but because they are suitable as an accompaniment, I include them here too.

Nutty Cauliflower Purée (Q)

(Serves 4-6)

This recipe gives a new dimension to cauliflower! The florets are cooked in stock and then puréed, mixed with mayonnaise and chopped toasted almonds. Serve hot. It really is gorgeous, it tastes so light and yet has a delicate crunch.

1 cauliflower, cut in florets
½-1 chicken or vegetable stock cube
Salt and freshly ground black pepper
2-3 tablespoons mayonnaise
40 g (1½ oz) toasted chopped almonds

To decorate:
toasted chopped almonds (about 15 g/½ oz)

Step 1: Cut a cross right into the stem of each floret, this helps them to cook quickly. Then cook them, barely covered in boiling water to which the stock cube has been added. (Don't be too generous with the water or the flavour of the stock cube will be too diluted). When just tender, drain off the liquid (use it in a soup). Purée the cauliflower in a food processor, or use a potato masher. It will not have a creamy smoothness but a nice 'grainy' looking texture. Season with salt and pepper if necessary. This much can be done the day before.

Step 2: Stir in the mayonnaise and almonds, reheat (to piping hot) in the saucepan and serve, sprinkled with remaining almonds.

Note: Ideally, all vegetables should be eaten as soon as prepared, however, when entertaining this point can be stretched somewhat!

Carrots in Orange Juice (Q)

(Serves 4-5)

Give your carrots a special touch. These flavours blend wonderfully. Can be made up the day before and reheated so ideal if entertaining.

700 g (1½ lb) carrots
Juice 2 oranges
4-5 cardamom pods
Salt and freshly ground black pepper
1 tablespoon finely chopped fresh parsley

Scrape the carrots and cut into 5-7.5 cm (2"-3") lengths. Slit these lengths in half down the centre, or in quarters or even in eights, if the carrots are very big. This gives you neat fingers of carrots. Steam the carrots (or boil) until just 'bite' tender. Drain.

Put the orange juice in a saucepan. Break open the cardamom pods and remove the black seeds which you add to the saucepan (discard the pods). Add some salt and pepper. Put in the carrots and heat everything gently together (with lid on) to allow flavours to mingle.

If you like, thicken the juice by adding **1 rounded teaspoon cornflour** blended with a small bit of water. Bring to the boil.

Serve sprinkled with the chopped parsley.

Quick Cooked Diced Potatoes (Q)

This is a great way to cook potatoes in a hurry. They are very flavoursome. The only nuisance bit is the preparation of the potatoes.

Peel and dice **1-2 potatoes per person** (or more!). Put in boiling water (use just barely enough to cover) to which **½-1 chicken stock cube** has been added. (If using a small amount, half a chicken stock cube will be plenty.) Cook until just tender. Drain off liquid (ideally use this liquid to make up a packet of soup or gravy). Put **2-3 tablespoons of olive oil** (or butter or margarine) into the saucepan. (If you have plenty of potatoes, you may need to increase this amount.) Add **2-4 cloves garlic,** crushed. Cook for a minute or two to soften. Then add in the drained potatoes along with very generous sprinklings of **chopped fresh parsley.** Toss everything together, season with a little **salt and freshly ground black pepper.**

Note: If you don't like garlic, use a small chopped onion instead.

Quick Courgettes (Q)

(Serves approx 3)

This is a delicious way to cook courgettes, making then lovely and moist and flavoursome. It cooks in a jiffy. Put **2-3 tablespoons of olive oil** into a frying pan and add **2 cloves garlic,** crushed. Fry for a minute or two. Cut the top and tail off **a medium/large courgette** (use about 350 g/12 oz for 3 servings), grate the courgette, unpeeled of course, into the pan. Season with **salt and freshly ground black pepper** and **½ teaspoon of sugar.** Also add a **few pinches of oregano** (or mixed herbs) and a **few pinches of nutmeg.** Fry, stirring frequently until the courgette mixture is nice and soft.

Serve fairly soon after cooking. (If left to sit for a long time, it gets a bit watery.)

Summer Medley (Q)

(Serves 3-4)

Lovely and juicy!

Wash **450 g (1 lb) small new potatoes.** Cook in a single layer in **300 ml (generous ½ pt) chicken stock.** The saucepan must not be too wide. When just tender add in **50 g (2 oz) each of frozen green beans and peas,** also **6 scallions** (chopped). Blend **1 heaped teaspoon cornflour** with a little water and add to the saucepan. Bring to boil to thicken. Season with **salt and freshly ground black pepper** and add **1-2 tablespoons chopped parsley.**

Buttered Peas with Garlic (Q)

(Serves 4-5)

Try these for flavour!

Melt **40 g (1½ oz) butter** (or use polyunsaturated margarine) in a saucepan and add about **2 cloves garlic** crushed. Also add **350 g (12 oz) frozen peas** - straight out of the packet! Cook gently stirring frequently until peas are thawed out and cooked. Season with **salt and freshly ground black pepper** (only takes about 10 minutes).

Potato and Mushroom Dish

(Serves 4-6)

This is rather like colcannon, but using mushrooms instead of cabbage or kale. Delicious.

900 g (2 lb) potatoes, peeled
175 g (6 oz) mushrooms, sliced
40 g (1½ oz) margarine
1-2 cloves garlic, crushed or chopped
Salt and freshly ground black pepper
1 onion, chopped finely
150 ml (¼ pt) milk
¼ teaspoon nutmeg
2 tablespoons chopped fresh parsley

Steam or boil the potatoes until tender. Mash them. While the potatoes are cooking, fry the mushrooms in the margarine until soft and juicy. Add the garlic and season with salt and pepper. In a separate little saucepan, cook the onion in the milk until soft.

When the potatoes are just mashed, add in the fried mushrooms, including all the lovely juices. Also add the milk and onion. Season with salt, pepper and nutmeg. Also add in the parsley. Mix everything together and put into a piping hot vegetable dish.

> **Capers** are flower buds of a bush native to the Mediterranean area. The dried buds are pickled in vinegar, giving a lovely sweet-sharp flavour. Usually sold in small jars

Caponata

(Serves 5-6)

If you like Ratatouille, chances are you'll love this Mediterranean dish also. It has a wonderful sweet/sour flavour and is equally good hot or cold. I love it with salmon and other dishes. Keeps well so it can be made in advance.

1 aubergine (about 275 g/10 oz)
1 small onion, chopped
8-10 tablespoons olive oil
3 sticks celery (225 g/8 oz), chopped
2-3 cloves garlic
4-5 tomatoes (about 275 g/10 oz), skinned and chopped
12 green olives (stones removed)
1 tablespoon capers, drained
Freshly ground black pepper
1 level teaspoon sugar
1-2 tablespoons vinegar (preferably wine vinegar)
Salt

See note on preparing aubergines on the next page.

Cook the onion in 2 tablespoons of the oil in a heavy based saucepan until soft. Add the celery and the garlic. Next add the tomatoes. Halve the olives and add to the saucepan along with the capers. (These ingredients may not always be in your press, but don't leave them out. They add special flavour to this dish.) Season with pepper and sugar. Add the vinegar. Cook gently with lid on.

Meanwhile, if not already prepared, chop the unpeeled aubergine into cubes (1.5 cm/¾" square). Put the remaining 6-8 tablespoons of olive oil into a frying pan and add the aubergine. Fry until golden brown. Transfer to the saucepan with the other vegetables. Cook until just soft. Season with salt, if necessary.

Note on Aubergines:
Many recipes suggest that after slicing or chopping, the unpeeled aubergine is put in a colander (or sieve) with salt scattered liberally over each layer. It is left for 1 hour covered with a plate. During this time a certain amount of liquid comes out. The aubergines are then rinsed under running water to remove the salt and juices and then patted dry. The reason for all this is to reduce the flavour of the aubergines. However, it is not essential and, I must admit, I rarely do it myself. Usually I only chop the aubergines just prior to frying as they often turn brown if left to stand.

Baked Courgettes

(Serves 5-6)

Sliced courgettes with mayonnaise and a little curry are baked in the oven. Makes an attractive vegetable dish.

350-450 g (¾-1 lb) courgettes, thinly sliced
60 ml (4 tablespoons) mayonnaise
90 ml (6 tablespoons) milk
1 level teaspoon curry powder
OR ½ teaspoon nutmeg
Salt and freshly ground black pepper
25 g (1 oz) melted margarine
2-3 tablespoons wholemeal breadcrumbs

Cooking Time: 20-30 minutes (200°C, 400°F, Gas 6).

Place the sliced courgettes in overlapping rows in an overproof dish. Whisk together the mayonnaise, milk, curry powder, salt and pepper. Pour over the courgettes.

Bake in the oven. After 15 minutes take out and brush visible slices with melted margarine and scatter with the breadcrumbs. Return to oven to make the tops slightly crispy. Serve hot.

Variation: Use half and half sliced courgettes and sliced tomatoes in the above recipe. Use only 45 ml (3 tablespoons of the milk.)

Cabbage and Pineapple Salad (Q)

(Serves 4-6)

Unusual but very effective combination of ingredients. Caraway seeds are reputed to make cabbage easy to digest!

275 g (10 oz) shredded cabbage (don't use dark leaves)
Tin pineapple chunks (400 g/14 oz), drained
1 small-medium onion
1-2 teaspoons caraway seeds
2 tablespoons chopped parsley

Dressing:
2 tablespoons vinegar
2 tablespoons pineapple juice
3-4 tablespoons oil
Salt and freshly ground black pepper
1 clove garlic, crushed

Shred the cabbage **very finely,** discarding thick stalks. (A food processor is great for this.) Wash and drain very well. Put into a bowl. Chop the pineapple quite small and also the onion. Add them to the cabbage along with caraway seeds and parsley.

Mix together the dressing ingredients and add as much as you like to the salad. Toss everything together. Season if necessary.

Mixed Salad with Fruit (Q)

(Serves 5-6)

Generous, colourful salads that include fruit and vegetables together are most attractive to look at and to eat!

1 head lettuce (see note)
3-4 tomatoes, roughly chopped
10 cm (4") length cucumber, unpeeled and roughly chopped
2 large bananas, sliced
1-2 eating apples, unpeeled and diced
150 g (5 oz) black grapes, cut in half and pips discarded
1 punnet (225 g/8 oz) strawberries (if available)
6 scallions (spring onions) OR 1 medium onion
2 tablespoons finely chopped fresh parsley

Dressing 1: Mix together
Juice 1 orange
2-3 tablespoons mayonnaise, or Greek style yogurt
OR
Dressing 2: Mix together

Juice ½ orange
1 tablespoon wine vinegar
2-3 tablespoons oil
Season with salt and freshly ground black pepper

Note: Chinese lettuce makes a good base for a salad instead of the standard lettuce (use about ½ head) or use a variety of lettuces, if you wish.

Wash, lightly dry and coarsely shred the lettuce and put into a salad bowl (wooden or glass).

Put the tomatoes, cucumber, bananas, eating apples, grapes, chopped strawberries and scallions in on top of the lettuce.

Mix the dressing of your choice and sprinkle over the salad, toss everything around, then sprinkle generously with the parsley.

Green Salad without Lettuce (Q)

(Serves 4)

Necessity is the mother of invention! Making a green salad one day, when I'd forgotten to buy lettuce, I put these ingredients together - much to my delight.

75 g (3 oz) mangetout
½ cucumber, unpeeled and chopped
1 bunch spring onions (scallions) washed
2 kiwi fruit
Salt and freshly ground black pepper

Dressing:
2 tablespoons mayonnaise
Juice ½ orange

To decorate:
1 tablespoon chopped fresh parsley

Put the mangetout in a bowl of cold water to refresh/crisp them. Drain. Trim each end and chop. Put into a salad bowl, add the cucumber. Slice the spring onions, peel and chop the kiwi and put them into the bowl also. Season with salt and pepper.

Mix the dressing ingredients and toss through the salad. Scatter with chopped fresh parsley.

Chill before serving.

Mediterranean Vegetable Mixture (Q)

This tasty vegetable mixture can be served on its own or used in the Vegetable Lasagne or the Vegetable Pancake recipes.

1 large onion, sliced thinly
2-4 cloves garlic, crushed or chopped
2-3 tablespoons olive oil
225 g (8 oz) mushrooms, sliced
1 medium courgette (275 g/10 oz), chopped
1 small red pepper (110 g/4 oz), chopped
1 small green pepper (110 g/4 oz), chopped
1 tin chopped tomatoes
Salt and freshly ground black pepper
1 level teaspoon oregano
2 teaspoons sugar
1 tablespoon tomato purée

Fry the onions and garlic in the oil until soft. Add all the other ingredients to the saucepan. Put the lid on and simmer gently until the vegetables are tender. (This takes about 20 minutes).

Cheese Sauce (Q)

Readily available in packets - but there is nothing to beat the flavour of the homemade one.

570 ml (1 pt) milk
75 g (3 oz) margarine
75 g (3 oz) flour
Salt and freshly ground black pepper
Slice of onion
1 level teaspoon mustard (grainy)
50 g (2 oz) grated cheddar cheese

Put all the ingredients, except the cheese, into a saucepan. Using a whisk, stir briskly over a moderate heat. Bring it to the boil, by which time you will have a nice smooth sauce. Add cheese and simmer, stirring until cheese melts.

Vegetable Pancakes (F)

(Serves approx. 6)

A most tasty meal!

9 pancakes, 20.5 - 23 cm (8" - 9") diameter (see note)
Mediterranean Vegetable Mixture (page 69)
570 ml (1 pt) cheese sauce (page 69)

Note: Use the Pancake recipe on page 53

Spread the vegetable mixture over the pancakes, roll them up. Place side by side in an ovenproof dish. Cover with cheese sauce. If everything is piping hot, serve as it is - if not, heat in the oven (190°C, 375°F, Gas 5) for about 25 minutes. If made up the day before, it will take about 45 minutes to heat through. Cover with foil if top gets too brown.

Serve hot.

Vegetable Lasagne (F)

(Serves 5-6)

The Mediterranean Vegetable mixture is so tasty - it makes an excellent filling.

Mediterranean Vegetable Mixture (as on page 69)
900 ml (1½ pt) cheese sauce (use 1½ times the
Cheese Sauce recipe) (page 69)
Lasagne sheets - enough to make 3 layers in the dish
50 g (2 oz) grated cheese (optional)

Dish: Lasagne dish 25.5 x 20.5cm (10" x 8").

Cooking time: About 40 minutes (190°C, 375°F, Gas 5). If Vegetable Lasagne is prepared in advance and is cold, it will take 15-20 minutes longer, reduce heat if necessary.

Pour a little cheese sauce in the base of the lasagne dish and put in a layer of lasagne sheets (not overlapping). Break to fit.

Pour in half the vegetable mixture and cover it with one quarter of the remaining cheese sauce. Arrange the second layer of lasagne on top. Pour in the remaining vegetable mixture and cover with one third of the remaining cheese sauce. Place the final layer of lasagne in position and cover with all the remaining cheese sauce. Sprinkle with cheese.

Bake until lasagne is cooked and the top is a lovely brown colour. Leave to stand for 15 minutes before serving.

Mushroom and Nut Loaf

(Serves 6)

This recipe is guaranteed to convert even the most hardened anti-vegetarian! It has a really delicious flavour and can be served hot or cold.

1 medium onion, finely chopped
50 g (2 oz) margarine
2-4 cloves garlic, crushed
450 g (1 lb) mushrooms, chopped
225 g (8 oz) wholemeal breadcrumbs
100 g (3½ oz) packet of chopped almonds or mixed nuts
Salt and freshly ground black pepper
½-1 level teaspoon dried oregano (or mixed herbs)
1 tablespoon chopped fresh parsley
2 eggs
1-2 teaspoons Worcester sauce OR soy sauce
OR 1 teaspoon Marmite

Tin: Loaf tin, 23 x 12.5 x 7.5 cm deep (9" x 5" x 3" deep)

Cooking Time: 50-60 minutes (190°C, 375°F, Gas 5).

Fry the onion in the margarine until soft, then add in the garlic. Add in the mushrooms and fry - unless you have a very large frying pan, you will probably need to do this in two lots. (If necessary, use an extra knob of margarine). The mushrooms are to be fried until they get nice and soft and reduced in volume. They don't need to brown.

Put the contents of the pan into a mixing bowl. Add the breadcrumbs and almonds. Season the mixture with salt and pepper and flavour with oregano and the parsley. In a separate jug, whisk together the eggs and Worcester sauce. (Marmite doesn't mix in easily.) Add to the mushroom mixture and mix well.

Turn into the prepared tin. Smooth out the top, brush with oil. Bake until nice and crusty on top and well set. Cover top with foil when it is brown enough.

Serve hot or cold.

Cauliflower with Tomato Sauce (Q)

(Serves 4-5)

Very tasty and colourful.

1 head cauliflower
2 tablespoons oil
1 small onion, chopped
2 rashers, chopped (optional)
1 clove garlic, crushed or chopped
1 tin chopped tomatoes
Salt and freshly ground black pepper
½ level teaspoon herbes de Provence (or oregano)
1 teaspoon sugar
3 level teaspoons cornflour blended with a little water

Break the head into florets and cut a cross in each stalk (to speed up cooking). Steam or boil in salted water until just tender. Meanwhile put the oil in a pan and fry the onion and rashers until rashers are crisp. Add in the remaining ingredients and mix well. Bring to the boil, stirring, to thicken somewhat. Pour over the cauliflower (drained) in a serving dish.

Savoury Rice and Fruit Salad

(Serves 5-6)

Brown (wholegrain) rice is my first choice - not only because it is more nutritious but because it also has a nice 'nutty' flavour. The fruit adds lovely colour to this salad.

2 small onions, chopped finely
2 tablespoons oil
1-2 cloves garlic, crushed or chopped
225 g (8 oz) rice (a heaped mugful)
2 full mugs (520 ml/18 fl oz) chicken stock (use a cube)
Salt and freshly ground black pepper
150 g (5 oz) black grapes
1-2 oranges
1-2 eating apples (preferably red skinned)
40-75 g (1½-3 oz) salted peanuts
2 sticks celery, thinly sliced
2 tablespoons chopped fresh parsley

Dressing:
4 tablespoons mayonnaise OR Greek Style yogurt
Juice ½-1 orange

To cook rice:
Add one of the small onions (the second one is for the salad itself) to the oil in a heavy based saucepan and fry gently to soften. Add the garlic and the rice, fry for a minute or two. Then add in the chicken stock. Season with salt and pepper (do this lightly if a stock cube has been used). Bring to the boil and simmer gently until the rice absorbs all the liquid - at which stage it will be tender (about 25-30 minutes). In the event of the rice not being tender, add a little boiling water (or stock) and continue cooking. Allow the rice to get cold.

Prepare the fruit and vegetables. Cut grapes in half and remove pips. (This may seem a bit tedious, but you'll be glad you did it when eating the salad). Peel the oranges with a sharp knife, cutting away the pith as well as the skin - to reveal the raw flesh. Cut out each section leaving the membrane (skin) behind. Wash and chop the unpeeled apples.

I like to add the dressing (mayonnaise mixed with enough orange juice to make it runny) to the cold cooked rice first, mixing it well through. Then I add the fruit, vegetables and the chopped parsley and mix them through. This way the dressing does not mask the lovely colours of the fruit and vegetables.

Variation: To make this into **a main dish,** add 350 g (12 oz) chopped cold meat (e.g. chicken, turkey, ham, pork etc.) and mix through.

Rooster is the name of a new type of potato developed in Ireland. The flesh is lovely and floury and they are so easy to peel. Nutritionally, the best way to cook potatoes is to steam them with their skins on.

Golden Potato and Cheese Cakes (Q)

(Serves about 4)

I often find it handy to cook quite a few potatoes at one time and so have them on standby to reheat at a moments notice, or to use in a recipe such as this delicious one!

Break **2 large eggs** in to a bowl and whisk lightly. Peel **450 g (1 lb) cooked potatoes** and grate them directly into the eggs. Melt **25 g (1 oz) margarine** in a pan and fry **1 onion** chopped finely and **1 clove garlic,** crushed, until they are soft. Add the contents of the pan to the egg mixture. Also add **50-75 g (2-3 oz) grated cheese** (preferably a mixture of cheddar and mozzarella). Season with **salt and freshly ground black pepper.** The mixture should be soft and eggy.

Fry in tablespoonfuls in a little oil or margarine until golden brown on both sides. Serve with a salad or with a mixed grill.

Spiced Rice with Fruit

(Serves 5-6)

This delightful combination of sweet and savoury makes a very tasty dish. Serve with pork, chicken or whatever you fancy!

2 tablespoons oil
1 small onion, chopped finely
1 small clove garlic, crushed
1 teaspoon grated fresh root ginger
225 g (8 oz) brown rice
1 chicken stock cube
2 mugs (520 ml/18 fl oz) water
50 g (2 oz) ready soaked dried apricots, chopped
50 g (2 oz) raisins
¼ teaspoon nutmeg
⅛ teaspoon cayenne pepper
¼ teaspoon coriander (optional)
Salt, if necessary
Freshly ground black pepper
Juice ½ lemon

To decorate:
40 g (1½ oz) toasted flaked almonds (optional)

Heat the oil in a saucepan. Add the onion and garlic and fry until soft, then add in the grated ginger. Next add in the rice, stock cube and water. Bring to the boil, cover with a lid and simmer gently for 15 minutes. Then add in all the remaining ingredients. Stir, cover with a lid and continue to simmer gently until rice is tender - about another 15 minutes.

Serve hot or cold scattered with almonds.

Bulgar is a cracked wheat that has been steamed. It compares loosely to brown/wholegrain rice - in that the outer bran has been removed, but the grain has not been polished. This leaves a lot of its natural goodness and fibre. Handy to have on your 'emergency shelf' as it needs no cooking, just steep in water. (See Bulgar Salad recipe.)

Bulgar Salad (Tabbouleh) (Q)

(Serves 5-6)

This salad is a speciality of the Lebanon. It contains lots of fresh parsley which is very rich in Vitamin C. If fresh mint is available, use it also. It has a wonderful green colour.

225 g (8 oz) bulgar
Boiling water or chicken stock to cover
4 rounded tablespoons chopped fresh parsley
5-6 spring onions (scallions), chopped
2-3 rounded teaspoons chopped fresh mint
OR 1 level teaspoon chopped mint in vinegar - i.e.mint sauce
2-3 tomatoes,skinned and chopped
Salt and freshly ground black pepper

Dressing:
3 tablespoons oil (preferably olive)
2 tablespoons lemon juice
1 clove garlic, crushed
Salt and freshly ground black pepper

Put the bulgar into a bowl and pour in enough boiling water (or chicken stock for a better flavour) to cover by a good 3.5 cm (1½"). (You can in fact use cold water, but then the steeping time is at least doubled.) When the bulgar has swollen and softened (about 15-25 minutes), drain off remaining water. Squeeze in a clean tea towel to dry as best as possible. Spread out to cool quickly, and when cold, put in a salad bowl. Add in the remaining ingredients. Season with salt and pepper if necessary. Put the dressing ingredients into a little bowl or jug to mix and then pour onto salad. Mix well together.

Variation: It is not traditional but you can make a main dish of the Tabbouleh by adding 1 carton (225 g/8 oz) cottage cheese to the finished mix and serve with crusty bread.

Bulgar Pilaff (Q)

(Serves 4-6)

This is equally delicious hot or cold. Serve instead of rice or potatoes. So quick to cook.

1 onion, chopped
1 clove garlic, crushed
2-3 tablespoons oil (preferably olive)
225 g (8 oz) bulgar
275 ml (½ pt) chicken stock
Salt and freshly ground black pepper
2-3 tomatoes, skinned and chopped
50 g (2 oz) peas

Fry the onion and garlic in the oil until soft. Next add the bulgar and chicken stock. Season with salt and pepper (salt not necessary if using stock cube). Bring to the boil, then cover and simmer gently for 5-10 minutes - just until the liquid has been absorbed. Add in the tomatoes and peas. Cook to heat through, if serving hot.

Pasta Salad (Q)

For ease of preparation and sheer ability to 'fill' one up, a pasta salad is hard to beat. It is especially great for outdoor eating like picnics and barbecues when everyone's appetite seems to double! The secret of a tasty salad is to cook the pasta in stock - I use a cube.

To cook pasta:
225 g (8 oz) pasta (twists, shells etc)
1 chicken stock cube
1 tablespoon oil

Dressing:
1 carton (125 ml) natural yogurt
2-4 tablespoons mayonnaise
Juice ½ orange
Salt and freshly ground black pepper
⅛ teaspoon nutmeg (optional)
OR 1 clove garlic crushed (optional)

Other ingredients:
1 small onion, finely chopped
2-3 stalks celery, chopped
110-175 g (4-6 oz) cooked ham, chopped
75 g (3 oz) salted peanuts
50-110 g (2-4 oz) black grapes
2 tablespoons chopped fresh parsley

Cook the pasta in plenty of boiling water with the stock cube and oil added. When 'bite' tender, drain thoroughly and cool. Pasta absorbs a lot of dressing. Mix the yogurt, mayonnaise and orange juice. Season with salt and pepper and flavour with nutmeg or garlic. This makes a good runny dressing. Mix enough of this through the cold pasta to coat evenly. Do this before adding the other ingredients, so dressing won't hide their colour.

Now add whatever else you fancy - I suggest the above ingredients onion, celery, cooked ham, peanuts and black grapes (do cut them in half and remove the pips). Mix through the pasta with some of the parsley, scattering the remainder of the parsley on top.

A recipe book dating back to 1360 recommends cooking pasta in stock instead of water! A stock cube is a convenient substitute. Raw pasta has the same approximate calorie content as white flour.

DESSERTS

(Q) = quick to cook   (F) = suitable for freezing

Strawberry Shortcake 78
Strawberries with Ogen Melon (Q) **79**
Baked Strawberry Tart 80
Plum Tart 81
Hungarian Apple Pudding 81
Poached Peaches (or Nectarines) with Fresh Basil (Q) **82**
Hot Spicey Pears (Q) **82**
Rhubarb Compôte (Stewed) (Q) **82**
Rhubarb and Orange Sponge (F) **83**
Blackberry Sponge (F) **84**
Luxury Mincemeat Pudding (F) **84**
Fluffy Orange Sauce (Q) **86**
Bananas with Orange and Cardamom (Q) **86**
Banana Ice Cream (F) **87**
Cranberry Cheesecake (F) **88**
Baked Cheesecake (with Mayonnaise) (F) **89**
Pavlova 90
Gateau Diane 91
Apple 'n Custard Ice Cream (F) **92**
Quick Brandy Baskets (Q) **93**
Brandy Snaps or Baskets 94

Historically desserts evolved because the housewife wanted to give a nourishing finish to a meal, using her eggs and fruit, especially if the main dish had been less than adequate. In our more prosperous times, a dessert is more often a treat rather than a necessity - especially as a lot of them are high in calories. However, a little of what you fancy does you good!

As much as possible I like to serve simple fresh fruit for desserts (as the French do). Try the Hungarian Apple Pudding for a delightful twist to an apple recipe. The Baked Strawberry (or Plum) Tarts are also good.

The build up of acids that cause tooth decay are at their strongest for about 30 minutes after eating. Therefore it is not the quantity of food and sugar that one eats (or drinks), but the number of times, that causes the most damage. (The acids from high sugar foods are also more intense!) Fibre in food is good in that it helps to scrape plaque off teeth as one chews.

Strawberry Shortcake

(Serves 5-6)

This classic American recipe really makes a punnet of strawberries go a long way! The shortcake is simply a sweet scone mixture, which is at its best when fresh.

Shortcake (Scone) Mixture:
225 g (8 oz) self raising flour
75 g (3 oz) caster sugar
75 g (3 oz) margarine
1 large egg yolk
120 ml (4 fl oz) milk (approx.)
½ teaspoon vanilla essence

Filling:
Punnet strawberries (225 g/8 oz)
Juice 1 orange
2 rounded teaspoons caster sugar
175-225 ml (6-8 fl oz) whipped cream, sweetened

Tin: Baking tin or sandwich tin 23 cm (9") diameter, greased.

Cooking Time: 30-40 minutes (190°C, 375°F, Gas 5)

Shortcake mixture: Put the flour and sugar into a bowl. Add the margarine (cut in lumps) and rub into the flour until like breadcrumbs (a food processor will do this in a minute). In a separate container, mix together the egg yolk, milk and vanilla essence. Add enough of this liquid to the dry ingredients to make a softish dough (i.e. not too stiff). Knead lightly on a floured surface and turn up the smooth underside. Press out into a circle about 18-20.5 cm (7-8") in diameter and about 1.5 cm (¾") deep. Place on the tin. Bake until golden brown and cooked through.

Meanwhile, prepare the strawberries. Pick out a few of the nicest ones to decorate the top and cut them into halves or quarters (I often leave the stalks on for added colour). Slice up the remaining strawberries and mix in the orange juice and sugar. Chill until required.

When the shortcake is baked, partly cool it on a wire tray. While still a little warm, slit it into two layers. The top layer will be smaller than the bottom layer. Spread the juicy strawberries over the bottom layer and cover with two-thirds of the whipped cream. Put the 'lid' (top layer) on, spread with the remaining cream and decorate with the halved strawberries.

Individual Strawberry Shortcakes

Using the exact same recipe, instead of making one shortcake, cut the prepared dough with a scone cutter and make individual scones. Bake in the same oven but the time will be shorter - about 20-25 minutes. When almost cool, slit scones and fill in the same way.

Sweet Scones (Q) (F)

Use the shortcake/scone mixture from the Strawberry Shortcake recipe. It makes 'melt-in-the-mouth' scones!

Make up as directed and cut the prepared dough (pressed a little thinner - 1 cm/½" thick) with a small scone cutter. Bake in the same temperature oven for about 20-25 minutes until golden and cooked through.

Serve with butter and jam, or cottage cheese and jam.

Strawberries with Ogen Melon

(Serves 4-5)

If you'd prefer to avoid the high calories of the above recipes, try this combination of flavours for a gorgeous dessert.

1 punnet (225 g/8 oz) strawberries
½ Ogen melon (discard pips, cut out of its skin)
Juice 1 orange
1 rounded teaspoon caster sugar

To decorate:
Mint leaves (optional)

It is important for this recipe that the strawberries and the melon have very good flavours. Chop or slice the strawberries and cut the melon into small chunks. Put them into a bowl with the orange juice and sugar. Chill and serve. Decorate with little sprigs of mint.

Baked Strawberry Tart

(Serves 6)

It is unusual to cook fresh strawberries as they lose their crisp freshness. But do try this tart - it is wickedly delicious. A great way to use strawberries that are not of such good quality.

The pastry case: You can use frozen shortcrust pastry (about 275 g/10 oz) or you can try this lovely Ground Almond Pastry.

150 g (5 oz) flour
50 g (2 oz) ground almonds
25 g (1 oz) caster sugar
75 g (3 oz) butter or margarine
3 tablespoons water (approx.)

Filling:
350 g (12 oz) of strawberries - (at a pinch 225 g/8 oz will do!)
50 g (2 oz) butter or margarine
50 g (2 oz) ground almonds
75 g (3 oz) caster sugar
1 level tablespoon cornflour
2 large eggs
Juice ½ orange
1 tablespoon liqueur or lemon juice

Tin: Sandwich tin, 23 cm (9") diameter, greased.

Cooking Time: About 20 minutes (200°C, 400°F, Gas 6) then reduce heat (190°C, 375°F, Gas 5) and cook for another 15-20 minutes (see note 1).

Pastry: Mix together the flour, ground almonds and caster sugar. Cut the butter into lumps and rub in until mixture looks like breadcrumbs. (This can be done in a food processor in a jiffy, see note 2). Add just enough water to make a dough - use a fork to mix. Knead lightly on a floured surface. If you have time allow pastry to 'rest' in the fridge for ½ hour, then roll out and line the tin.

Filling: Cut strawberries in half and place, cut side down, in a tight layer all over the pastry base. Melt the butter. Take off the heat. Add in all the remaining ingredients and whisk together. Pour over the strawberries. Bake until well cooked and a nice deep golden brown.

Serve warm or cold.

80

Note 1: If you prefer you can cook the empty pastry case in the hot oven first. This will take about 20 minutes. Pierce the base making a number of tiny holes, using a fork, before baking. Check after 10 minutes - if the base is rising up in a big bump, pierce it with a sharp pointed knife to release the air so it will be nice and flat again! When cooked, put in filling and bake at the lower temperature for about half an hour. This method ensures a well cooked pastry case!

Note 2: If using a food processor - watch carefully - if overdone the margarine is softened and turns into a dough.

Plum Tart

(Serves 6)

Fresh plums (450 g/1 lb) can be used instead of the strawberries in the Baked Strawberry Tart recipe. Omit the lemon juice and instead add **½ teaspoon almond essence** and **¼ teaspoon cinnamon.**

The plums are cut in half. The stone will remain in one half. I find, unless the plums are ripe, it is impossible to remove the stone without making a botch of the half plum - so I just leave them in! I tell everyone to watch for the stones!

Hungarian Apple Pudding

(Serves 5-6)

Grated apple, beaten egg whites and orange juice combine to make a delightful, light tasting dessert.

25 g (1 oz) margarine
150 g (5 oz) caster sugar
2 large eggs, separated
3 large cooking apples, peeled (700-900 g/1½-2 lbs)
1 mug (65 g/2½ oz) breadcrumbs (brown or white)
Juice 2 oranges
½ level teaspoon nutmeg

Dish: Ovenproof dish, 1.75 litre size (3 pt) size, greased. Stand it in a tin (or larger dish) of water. (This ensures that the pudding cooks at a nice even pace).

Cooking Time: 50-60 minutes (180°C, 350°F, Gas 4)

Put the margarine into a mixing bowl and mix to soften. Beat in 50 g (2 oz) of the caster sugar and the egg yolks. Grate the apples into this mixture and then add in the bread-crumbs, orange juice and nutmeg. Mix all together.

In a separate bowl, whisk the egg whites until fluffy. Then gradually beat in the remaining sugar until the mixture is quite stiff - though not as completely stiff as a meringue mixture. Stir this egg white mixture through the apple mixture - gently but thoroughly.

Turn into the prepared dish and bake. When cooked the top is nicely browned. As the pudding is moist, it is not essential to serve cream or sauce with it.

Poached Peaches (or Nectarines) with Fresh Basil (Q)

(Serves 3-4)

Under ripe peaches can be made deliciously tender if poached. For **6 peaches,** use **juice of 2 oranges** and nearly **150 ml (¼ pt) water.** Put the water and orange juice in a little saucepan along with about **75 g (3 oz) caster sugar.** Stir gently until the sugar is dissolved. Add the peaches with their skins on (this gives lovely pink colour to the syrup). Poach gently until just tender. Finely chop **3-4 leaves of fresh basil** and add to the syrup.

Serve warm or chilled.

Variation: Add **½ teaspoon cinnamon** to the water and orange juice.

Hot Spicey Pears (Q)

(Serves 3)

Turn a tin of pears into a hot dessert in a jiffy.

Empty a **tin of pear halves** (including the juice) into a saucepan. Add **¼ teaspoon each of ground nutmeg and cinnamon** and **2 whole cloves.** You can in fact be more generous with these spices if you like. Also add the **juice of half a lemon** and **a little sugar** to taste. Bring to the boil and then simmer gently, with the lid on, for a few minutes. Serve hot with a little cream or ice cream. These pears are equally nice eaten cold.

Rhubarb Compôte (Stewed) (Q)

(Serves 3-4)

Quick and light tasting rhubarb cooked in a sugar syrup.

1 large bunch rhubarb
75 ml (⅛ pint) water
75 g (3 oz) sugar
Juice 1-2 oranges
Generous pinches of cinnamon

Top and tail the rhubarb stalks, wash and cut into 2.5 cm (1") lengths.

Put the water and sugar into a saucepan over a moderate heat until the sugar dissolves. Add the orange juice and the rhubarb, put a lid on the saucepan and simmer gently until the rhubarb is tender but hasn't lost its shape (keep the lid on as much as possible to prevent evaporation).

Turn the rhubarb into a hot dish and sprinkle with cinnamon. This recipe is also nice served cold.

Variation: Include two oranges, peeled with a sharp knife to remove skin and pith, then cut into slices. Add to rhubarb when nearly tender.

Microwave: This recipe is ideal for the microwave. Omit the water. Just add orange juice and sugar and cook in a dish for 6-7 minutes until tender, then sprinkle with the cinnamon

Rhubarb and Orange Sponge (F)

(Serve 5-6)

A simple recipe, sponge topping on rhubarb, is made extra special by including orange juice. A hearty dessert like this is excellent after a light meal.

450 g (1 lb) rhubarb (medium sized bunch)
100 g (3½ oz) sugar (brown or white)
Grated rind and juice of 1 orange

Sponge:
75 g (3 oz) self raising flour
50 g (2 oz) wholemeal flour
110 g (4 oz) margarine
110 g (4 oz) caster sugar
2 large eggs

Cooking Time: About 45 minutes (190°C, 375°F, Gas 5)

Top and tail the rhubarb stalks, wash and cut into pieces 2.5 cm (1") long and put into an ovenproof dish. Sprinkle the sugar, orange juice and rind over the rhubarb.

Mix the flours together in a separate container. Put the margarine and sugar into a bowl and beat together until light and fluffy. Then beat in the eggs one at a time, adding a little of the mixed flours with each one. Then stir in the rest of the mixed flours. Drop this mixture in small spoonfuls all over the rhubarb and spread out evenly, if you can. But don't worry, it will spread out itself during the cooking. Place in the oven and cook until baked right through. Pierce the centre with a knife, if no doughy particles cling to the knife, the sponge is cooked. This is important because it takes time for the centre to cook. If getting too brown, reduce the oven heat.

Serve hot or cold.

Blackberry Sponge (F)

(Serves 5-6)

Even if you don't have time to pick the blackberries yourself - do a ramble round your supermarket freezer cabinets and you should find bags of frozen blackberries. They are very good. (I love to include some in my apple tarts.)

Use **350 g (12 oz) of frozen blackberries** instead of the rhubarb in the above recipe. Use only **50 g (2 oz) white sugar** to sweeten them. They can be used from frozen.

Luxury Mincemeat Pudding (F)

(Serves 6-8)

Delicious - especially when served with Fluffy Orange Sauce. This pudding can be eaten on the day of cooking or it will keep for about 2-3 weeks. Suitable for Christmas or anytime.

Using self raising flour and baking powder results in a lovely spongy pudding. If you would prefer the more traditional close textured pudding, use ordinary flour and leave out the baking powder (NOT the bread soda).

Mixing Bowl 1:
2 cartons (100 g/3½ oz each) mixed peel
2 cartons (100 g/3½ oz each) glacé cherries
50 g (2 oz) chopped or flaked almonds
2 mugs brown breadcrumbs (175 g/6 oz)
110 g (4 oz) brown sugar (demerara)
150 g (5 oz) self raising flour
1 level teaspoon each nutmeg, cinnamon and ground cloves
1 level teaspoon each baking powder and bread soda

Turkey in orange juice sauce

Almond feather sponge and macaroons

Fish pastry parcels

Plum tart

Mixing Bowl 2:
Jar of mincemeat (450 g/1 lb)
2 eggs, beaten
1 cup milk (175 ml/6 fl oz)
Small glass Whiskey (about 50 ml/2 fl oz)
Juice half a lemon
110 g (4 oz) melted margarine

1 pudding bowl 1.75 litre (3 pint) well buttered inside.

Cooking Time: Steam Bake for 3-4 hours in oven (150°C, 300°F, Gas 2) (see directions below). Steam baking is very convenient because the steam is in the oven - not in the kitchen. However, it is important that the water **never** evaporates or the plastic (polypropylene) bowl will melt. If you'd prefer to be on the safe side, use a pyrex or delph pudding bowl

Steaming can be done in traditional manner in a steamer or in a pressure cooker if you prefer. The time is the same for traditional steaming. For pressure steaming follow directions in the instruction book.

Mix together all the ingredients in mixing bowl 1. Do likewise with mixing bowl 2.

Now add the wet ingredients (bowl 2) into the dry ingredients (bowl 1). Mix well and turn into the prepared pudding bowl.

Steam Bake: Cover the top of the bowl with a double layer of greaseproof paper, which is greased on the side nearest to the pudding, and has a pleat/fold across the centre (to allow for expansion). Tie the paper securely with string around the rim of the bowl. Cover the top of the bowl again with a double layer of foil (not tied). This is to prevent the pudding cooking like a cake in the oven.

Stand the covered pudding bowl in a large cake tin or roasting tin. Place the two of them right into a turkey roasting bag (with no holes!). Fill the tin three quarters full with very hot water. Close the turkey bag leaving a very small opening for the steam to escape. Put the turkey roasting bag and its contents on a flat baking tin. This protects the roasting bag from being damaged. Cook in the oven.

Check the level of water during cooking. It will be easy to see through the roasting bag. Top up, if necessary, with boiling water. Be very careful lifting the tin in and out of the oven. (The turkey roasting bag can be re-used a number of times for this.)

When cooked, serve or store. If storing it (maximum of 3 weeks), cover with fresh greaseproof paper and store in a cool airy place. The pudding can be frozen.

If liked, a little whiskey or brandy can be trickled onto the surface of the pudding for extra flavour.

Fluffy Orange Sauce (Q)

This delicious sauce really adds a special mmm...! to the Luxury Mincemeat Pudding. Indeed it can be used to liven up any dessert of your choice.

25 g (1 oz) margarine (or butter)
Grated rind and juice 1 orange
A little water
1 level teaspoon flour
50 g (2 oz) caster sugar
1 large egg, separated
Juice of half a lemon

Soften the margarine (mash on plate or soften in a microwave). Mix in the grated orange rind, the flour and the sugar, as well as the egg yolk. Transfer to a small saucepan.

Add enough water to the juice of the orange to make up 150 ml (5 fl oz) and blend into the mixture in the saucepan (don't mind if it looks curdled at this stage). Bring to the boil to thicken. Take it off heat.

Whisk the egg white until very stiff and mix gently into the orange mixture while it is still warm, also mix in the lemon juice. These give the sauce its lovely fluffy consistency and its delicious piquant flavour.

Serve warm or cold.

Bananas with Orange and Cardamom (Q)

(Serves 4-6)

This makes a special dessert of bananas. Interestingly, the banana plant is a distant relative of the ginger and cardamom. Maybe this is why these flavours are so nice together.

4-5 bananas
25 g (1 oz) margarine
Grated rind and juice 1 large orange
1 tablespoon of honey OR sugar
1 teaspoon grated fresh root ginger
2-4 pods of cardamom

Cooking Time: These can be cooked in a wide saucepan for about 10 minutes OR for 20 minutes in the oven (190°C, 375°F, Gas 5).

Peel the bananas and slit in two. Lay side by side in an ovenproof dish.

Melt the margarine in a saucepan and add the orange rind and cook very gently for a minute or two. Add the orange juice, honey and ginger. Crush open the cardamom pods and only add the little black seeds to the mixture (discard pods). Bring to the boil and pour over the bananas.

Cover loosely with foil and bake until the bananas are just soft.

To cook in a saucepan: Choose a wide based saucepan. Cut the bananas to fit. Cook in the prepared mixture.

Delicious on their own but cream or ice-cream can be served with them.

Banana Ice cream (F)

(Serves 5-6)

For a delicious smooth ice cream, use the recipe for Bananas with Orange and Cardamom. Mash into a purée and mix with **275 ml (½ pt) whipped cream.** Also add the **juice of ½ lemon.** Use this mixture to make ice cream (see page 92).

Nutritional Note: Bananas are a good source of potassium, before ripening they are rich in starch (some countries use them as a vegetable at this stage). After ripening, the starch turns to sugar.

Cranberry Cheesecake ('F)

(Serves 8)

Even though fresh cranberries are only available near Christmas time, I am including this recipe because it is so tasty! The flavour is sharp and sweet and the colour is a rich pink. The cranberry purée will freeze for 3-4 months.

Base:
225 g (8 oz) digestive biscuits
110 g (4 oz) margarine or butter, melted

Cranberry purée:
1 packet fresh cranberries (350 g/12 oz)
75 g (3 oz) sugar

Cheese mixture:
200 g (7 oz) cream cheese
225 g (8 oz) cottage cheese
1 packet raspberry jelly (570 ml/1 pt size) (see note)

Tin: Use round tin, 23 cm (9") diameter with removable base, lightly oiled.

Base: Crush the biscuits into fine crumbs (in a food processor or place them in a bag and bash them with a rolling pin). Add melted butter and spread mixture evenly over base of tin. Chill.

Cranberry Purée: Put the cranberries into a saucepan with enough water to just cover them, 300 ml (a generous ½ pint). Put the lid on and bring to the boil, then simmer gently until cranberries are tender. Add the sugar to them. Press the cranberries through a colander (or a sieve) - I use a colander because its holes are larger and they allow more fruit through (without the skin).

Put the cream cheese and cottage cheese into a food processor and buzz until smooth. (If no food processor is available, simply sieve the cottage cheese before mixing with the cream cheese.)

Dissolve the jelly in about 150 ml (¼ pint) water. Allow to cool. Add to the cheese mixture with the cranberry purée. Mix well and pour into the prepared base. Allow to cool in the fridge for a few hours.

Note: The texture of this cheesecake is a little softer than a normal one. If you wish it to be stiffer (e.g. for a buffet), dissolve ½ sachet gelatine with the jelly.

Baked Cheesecake (with Mayonnaise) (F)

(Serves 6-8)

The mayonnaise and lemon juice give a nice 'tangy' flavour. Baked in the oven, it is served cool or chilled. Using cottage cheese helps keep the calories down.

Base:
225 g (8 oz) digestive biscuits
110 g (4 oz) butter or margarine, melted
15 g (½ oz) caster sugar

Cheese mixture:
2 x 225 g (8 oz) cartons cottage cheese
Carton (125 ml) natural yogurt
8 level tablespoons (120 ml) mayonnaise
75 g (3 oz) caster sugar
Finely grated rind 1 lemon
4 tablespoons lemon juice
1 teaspoon vanilla essence
2 eggs

Tin: Use round tin 23 cm (9") diameter with removable base.

Cooking Time: 45-55 minutes (170°C, 325°F, Gas 3)

Crush the digestive biscuits into fine crumbs and blend with the melted butter and sugar and press in an even layer on the base of the tin.

Put the cottage cheese into a food processor and add in the yogurt, mayonnaise, sugar, lemon juice, rind, vanilla essence, and the eggs. 'Buzz' everything together until smooth and creamy.

(If you don't have a food processor, press the cottage cheese through a sieve to smooth out the lumps. Put into a bowl and mix in the other ingredients.)

Pour cheese mixture into the prepared tin. Bake until set and golden. After turning off the oven, leave the cheesecake to set in the oven for another hour. Take out and cool completely.

Serve on its own or with fresh fruit salad. Good, isn't it.

Pavlova

(Serves 6)

The ever popular dessert. The secret of good meringue is to beat in the sugar a little at a time. The pavlova will have a soft centre.

Meringue base:
3 large egg whites
175 (6 oz) caster sugar
1 rounded teaspoon cornflour
1 teaspoon lemon juice (or vinegar)

To decorate:
3-4 kiwi fruits (see note)
2-3 oranges
175-250 ml (6-9 fl oz) cream
1 tablespoon caster sugar

Note: Any choice of fruit can be used.

Tin: Mark a circle 20.5-23 cm (8-9") diameter on a sheet of baking parchment and place it on a baking tin.

Cooking Time: About 1-2 hours (140°C, 275°F, Gas 1) until well crisped on the outside. Ovens can vary a lot at low temperatures so adjust yours if necessary. The colour of the pavlova should be nearly white or at most a very pale gold.

Put the egg whites into a very clean bowl and whisk until just stiff. Then add the sugar - half a tablespoon at a time. Beat the mixture between each addition of sugar. The result will be a very stiff mixture that won't move if the bowl is turned upside down. The cornflour and lemon juice can be added to the mixture with the last spoon of sugar.

Spoon the meringue mixture out onto the prepared baking parchment, and shape into a circle - a bit more shallow in the centre. If you want it to be really special, hold back some of the meringue mixture, put into an icing bag with a rose pipe, and pipe "roses" of meringue all around the edge of the circle. Cook until crisp.

Cool on a wire tray and peel off the baking parchment very carefully. Store the meringue base in an airtight container until required. (It will keep 4-5 days).

To decorate: Peel and thinly slice the kiwi fruit. If the slices are large, cut them in half. Cut the skin off the oranges with a sharp knife, removing the pith and also revealing the juicy flesh. Cut into thin slices. Whip the cream until stiff and sweeten with the sugar. Spread over the meringue base and arrange the fruit in overlapping slices over the top.

Gateau Diane

This is a great special occasion dessert. For larger numbers (10-12) double the ingredients.

Meringue:
4 large egg whites
225 g (8 oz) caster sugar or icing sugar
75 g (3 oz) finely chopped almonds (optional)

Chocolate Cream:
110 g (4 oz) dark cooking chocolate (good quality)
350 ml (12 fl oz) cream
1-2 tablespoons fresh orange juice (OR a liqueur)

To decorate:
Fresh strawberries and/or chocolate craque (see below) or
grated chocolate (50 g/2 oz)

Tins: Mark out three circles 20.5 cm (8") diameter on three pieces of baking parchment and place these on baking tins. If your serving plate is a different shape, you can mark out that shape (three times) instead. For larger numbers use 25.5 (10") circles.

Cooking Time: About 2 hours (120°C, 250°F, Gas ½)

To make the meringue
Whisk the egg whites until frothy. Add the sugar, a little at a time, beating in each addition. When mixture is stiff enough not to come out when bowl is upside down, it is ready. Don't continue beating as it can make the meringue lose its stiffness.

Divide the mixture between the three pieces of paper and spread out to fit the circle (or other shape). Smooth surface and scatter with almonds. Cook until well dried out and only a very pale colour. Allow to cool.

These can be made in advance and kept in an airtight bag or tin for a few days.

Chocolate Cream:
Put the chocolate into a bowl with the orange juice or liqueur. Also add 3 tablespoons of the cream. Melt these together. Avoid stirring until chocolate is melted through. Then stir and allow to cool somewhat. Half whip the remaining cream, add the chocolate mixture and whip for a minute or so to mix - which will also stiffen the cream.

Assemble the gateau:
Do not assemble until the day of serving. Spread some of the chocolate cream between the layers of the meringue sitting on the serving plate. Cover top and sides with the remaining cream.

Sprinkle with grated chocolate or decorate with chocolate craque.

If available, decorate also with fresh strawberries (optional).

Chocolate Craque (Curls): Melt **110 g (4 oz) chocolate** and pour onto a cold surface. Spread out to about 1 cm (½") thick. Allow to cool but **not** get cold. Use a sharp knife to draw (or scrape) the surface towards you. A thin layer of chocolate will curl up. Continue until you have lots of curls.

Apple 'n' Custard Ice Cream (F)

(Serves 5-6)
This makes a delightful fresh tasting ice cream. For special occasions, serve in Brandy Baskets (page 93 and 94)

Custard:
2-3 large egg yolks
1 level tablespoon caster sugar
¼ teaspoon vanilla essence
150 ml (¼ pt) milk
150 ml (¼ pt) cream (see note)

275 ml (½ pt) stewed apples, sweetened

Note: Use 275 ml (½ pt) cream if you wish, omitting milk.

Make the custard: Put the egg yolks into a bowl with the sugar and vanilla. Heat the cream and the milk in a little saucepan but do not boil. Pour onto the egg yolks, whisking briskly. Return mixture to the saucepan and cook over a gentle heat, stirring continuously until custard is thick enough to coat the back of a wooden spoon.

Add the custard to the stewed apples and mix well together. Use this mixture to make ice cream.

To Make Ice Cream
Set the dial of the freezer to "quick freeze" 1 hour before hand (or set fridge to highest setting).

Prepare the ice cream mixture as directed. Place it, in a bowl, in the freezer or ice box and leave to get half frozen (mushy). Remove bowl from freezer and whisk thoroughly with rotary or electric beater. This is to break down big ice crystals and so make a smoother ice cream. Turn mixture into container in which you wish to freeze ice cream - and freeze completely.

The secret of a successful **meringue** (one that does not weep out a lot of sticky syrup while it cooks) is the rate at which the sugar is beaten into the egg whites. It must be added gradually, beating well as you go.

Ginger is highly valued in Eastern cooking and was used medicinally before it became a condiment.

Quick Brandy Baskets (Q)

A pretty way to serve some desserts (such as ice cream) is in individual little 'baskets' made from Brandy Snaps. This is a very quick method!

Buy a **packet of Brandy Snaps!** Put the Brandy Snaps, two at a time on a tin, into a moderate oven (180°C, 350°F, Gas 4) for about 2 minutes to soften them. Unroll the Brandy Snap and place over an orange (or over the bottom of a tumbler) to shape into a basket (bowl) shape with wavy edges. As soon as it cools it sets in this shape. These make small little baskets. If you'd prefer larger ones, you'll have to make up the mixture yourself! The recipe is on the next page.

Brandy Snaps or Baskets

Each brandy snap or basket must be shaped while still hot from the oven. Only cook 2-3 at one time. Have two tins, so that one lot can be cooking while another lot is being shaped.

110 g (4 oz) margarine or butter
110 g (4 oz) brown sugar (demerara)
110 g (4 oz) golden syrup (see note)
3 teaspoons brandy
¼ teaspoon vanilla essence
110 g (4 oz) flour
1 rounded teaspoon ground ginger
1 teaspoon lemon juice

Tins: Non-stick baking tins, greased lightly.

Cooking Time: About 4-8 minutes (180°C, 350°F, Gas 4)

Gently heat the butter, sugar and syrup together in a saucepan until the sugar melts. Cool slightly. Add the brandy and vanilla essence. Sift the flour and ginger into a bowl and mix the melted ingredients into them as well as the lemon juice.

Put teaspoonfuls (2-3 together) at least 10 cm (4") apart on a greased tin and bake until biscuits are bubbly and lacy in texture and golden brown. Leave on tin for a minute or two to stiffen, then lift off with a sharp knife or egg lifter and immediately shape as required.

Brandy Snaps: Wrap around the handle of a greased wooden spoon (with bumpy side out). Allow to cool partly on the spoon - ideally have 3 wooden spoons in use so each brandy snap has time to cool quickly on the handle while you roll the next.

To serve - pipe whipped, sweetened cream into centre.

Brandy Baskets - shape over bottom of a drinking glass (greased) (use 2 at a time). When cold store in an airtight tin or plastic bag. Fill as required immediately before serving.

Note: Stand the tin of golden syrup on the scales and remove 110 g (4 oz) out of it!

BREAD AND CAKES

(Q) = Quick to cook   (F) = Suitable for freezing

High sugar foods release energy (glucose) quickly into the blood stream - which is followed by a corresponding drop. The ideal way to eat sugar is combined with fibre, because this ensures a nice even flow of energy into the blood stream. Happily lots of my favourite cake recipes are also rich in fibre. The Fruity Carrot Loaf has wholemeal flour, dried fruits, nuts and carrots all providing fibre. However since the occasional splurge doesn't do much harm. I love to indulge myself with Chocolate Yogurt Cake or Macaroons to name but two!

(Unfortunately ovens vary, so cooking temperatures may need to be adjusted accordingly.)

Wholemeal Herb and Cheese Scones (Q) (F)

These have a lovely savoury flavour. Delicious with soups or salads.

225 g (8 oz) self raising flour
225 g (8 oz) wholemeal flour
1 rounded teaspoon baking powder
½ teaspoon salt
lots of freshly ground black pepper
50 g (2 oz) margarine
2 tablespoons chopped fresh parsley
2 tablespoons chopped onion or chives (optional)
½-1 teaspoon of mixed herbs
110 g (4 oz) grated cheese (optional)
2 large eggs
Generous 150 ml (¼ pt) milk
1 teaspoon of mustard (use if adding cheese)

Tin: Baking tin(s), greased.

Cooking Time: 20-30 minutes (200°C, 400°F, Gas 6).

Put the flours, baking powder, salt and pepper into a bowl. Rub in the margarine until like breadcrumbs. Add parsley, onion and mixed herbs. Then mix in the grated cheese.

In a separate container, mix together eggs, milk and mustard. Add enough liquid to the dry ingredients to make a softish dough. Turn out onto a floured surface. Knead lightly, turn up smooth underside and shape into a square or rectangle. Cut into square scones (about 5 cm/2"). Bake on greased tin(s) until well risen, golden brown and cooked through.

Variation: Before baking, brush scones with milk and scatter with sesame seeds.

Brown Bread Loaf (F)

This recipe bakes the brown bread in a loaf tin, rather than in the traditional round shape. They can be frozen so why not make two at a time! The hazelnut yogurt gives a subtle flavour to the bread. Very suitable for fan ovens.

225 g (8 oz) wholemeal flour
225 g (8 oz) self raising flour
1 rounded teaspoon of baking powder
1 level teaspoon bread soda

1 carton (125 ml) yogurt with hazelnuts
1 large egg
Fresh milk - about 225 ml (8 fl oz)

To decorate: sesame seeds (optional)

Tin: Loaf Tin 23 cm x 12.5 cm x 7.5 cm (9" x 5" x 3" deep) well greased.

Cooking Time: About 50-60 minutes (190°C, 375°F, Gas 5), reduce heat (180°C, 350°F, Gas 4) after about 15 minutes.

Put the first 4 ingredients into a bowl and mix together. Put the yogurt and egg into a bowl. Add the milk. Whisk together. Add to the dry ingredients to make a soft dough.

Turn into the tin. Smooth top and scatter with sesame seeds and bake until cooked through. Partly cool in the tin and turn out onto a wire tray.

Fruity Carrot Loaf (F)

A favourite recipe of mine. Also excellent in lunch boxes. The dried fruit and nuts are really good in this carrot cake mixture, giving extra nourishment, fibre and flavour.

110 g (4 oz) wholemeal flour
175 g (6 oz) self raising flour
1 heaped teaspoon baking powder
2 level teaspoons nutmeg
2 level teaspoons cinnamon
100 g (3½ oz) carton mixed peel
110 g (4 oz) raisins
50 g (2 oz) chopped walnuts
110 g (4 oz) margarine
110 g (4 oz) brown sugar (demarara)
225 g (8 oz) grated carrots
2 large eggs (size 1)
Milk, if necessary

Tin: Loaf tin 23 cm x 12.5 cm x 7.5 cm deep (about 9" x 5" x 3" deep)

Cooking Time: About 1¼ - 1½ hours (180°C, 350°F, Gas 4).

Put the flours, baking powder and spices into a bowl. Mix in the dried fruit and nuts.

Melt the margarine. Take off the heat and stir in the sugar and carrot. Break the eggs into these "wet" ingredients and mix them all together.

Stir the "wet" ingredients into the dry ones to make a fairly soft mixture. (If necessary, add a little milk.)

Pour into the prepared tin, smooth top and bake until cooked through.

Partly cool in the tin, standing it on a wire tray. Then turn out and cool completely.

Nutritional Note: Carrots were traditionally used to sweeten cakes. They are wonderfully low in calories and contain lots of fibre as well as being a good source of Vitamin A. The dried fruit contains natural sugar and fibre.

Fruit and Nut Roll

Shaped rather like a squat Vienna roll and baked on a flat tin, this fruity roll is much more delicious than its simple ingredients would suggest.

350 g (12 oz) self raising flour
110 g (4 oz) caster sugar
110 g (4 oz) margarine
½-1 teaspoon each nutmeg and cinnamon
225 g (8 oz) raisins
100 g (3½ oz) carton mixed peel
100 g (3½ oz) packet walnuts, chopped
2 eggs, beaten lightly
Milk, use enough when added to the eggs to measure 175 ml
(6 fl oz), approx.
½ teaspoon vanilla essence

Tin: Greased baking tin.

Cooking Time: About 45-60 minutes. (180°C, 350°F, Gas 4).

Put the flour and sugar into a bowl. Rub in the margarine until like fine breadcrumbs. (This can be done in a food processor). Add the spices, fruit and nuts to the flour, mix together. In a separate bowl, mix the milk, eggs and vanilla essence.

Stir the liquid ingredients into the dry ones, mixing well to make a dough that is not too stiff. Add a little more milk if necessary. Turn this dough out onto a floured surface and knead just a little. Turn up the smooth underside and shape into an oval (somewhat like a Vienna roll), about 5 cm (2") thick. Put onto the tin. Bake in the oven until cooked through. Cover with foil when it is brown enough. Test centre with a skewer.

Cool on a wire tray. Dust with icing sugar. Serve sliced, with or without butter.

Caraway Seed Cake (F)

Caraway seeds are quite easily obtained on a well stocked spice rack. Keep a day or two before cutting.

175 g (6 oz) butter or margarine
175 g (6 oz) caster sugar
juice 1 small lemon
275 g (10 oz) self-raising flour
4 eggs
3-4 level teaspoons caraway seeds

Tin: Round cake tin 20.5 cm (8") diameter lined with greaseproof paper OR loaf tin 23 x 12.5 x 7.5 cm (9" x 5" x 3" deep), greased and dusted with flour.

Cooking Time: About 1 hour (180°C, 350°F, Gas 4)

Cream the butter with the sugar and the lemon juice until light and fluffy. Then beat in the eggs one at a time adding a little of the flour with each one. Stir in the caraway seeds and the rest of the flour. Turn the cake mixture into the prepared tin.

Bake until cooked through. Test centre with a skewer which should come out clean. When baked, leave it in the tin standing on a wire tray for about 15 minutes before gently turning out to cool completely.

Variation: Substitute 50 g (2 oz) of the flour with ground almonds.

Carrot and Pineapple Cake

This delicious moist cake is American inspired. The oil and pineapple make it wonderfully moist.

175 ml (6 fl oz) corn or vegetable oil
110 g (4 oz) caster sugar
110 g (4 oz) brown sugar (demerara)
3 large eggs
½ teaspoon vanilla essence
175 g (6 oz) self raising flour
2 teaspoons cinnamon
1 teaspoon nutmeg
175 g (6 oz) grated carrots
150 g (5 oz) crushed pineapple, drained
1½ tablespoons pineapple juice
50-110 g (2-4 oz) chopped walnuts or almonds

Tin: Loaf tin 23 cm x 12.5 cm x 7.5 cm deep (9" x 5" x 3") - well greased.

Cooking Time: About 1-1½ hours (180°C, 350°F, Gas 4)

Mix the first 5 ingredients together. Sift the flour and spices into another bowl. Stir in the liquid mixture adding in the carrots, pineapple and nuts. Mix well and put into the prepared tin.

Bake until cooked through, test with a skewer to see if centre is cooked.

Cool in the tin, standing on a wire tray.

Orange Icing

From a calorie point of view, I try to avoid using icing - but my family say the cake is not complete without it.

50 g (2 oz) cream cheese (light!)
175 g (6 oz) icing sugar
1-3 tablespoons fresh orange juice

Soften the cream cheese by stirring in a bowl. Mix in icing sugar and enough orange juice to make a stiffish icing or put all in a food processor and "buzz" . Spread over top of the cake.

Chocolate and Yogurt Cake

A really special chocolate cake - dark, moist and rich. Ideal also as a dessert. Natural yogurt is the 'secret' ingredient.

(Weigh ingredients carefully).

40 g (1½ oz) cocoa
6 tablespoons hot water
1 carton (125 ml) natural yogurt
190 g (6½ oz) flour, NOT self raising
½ level teaspoon bread soda
1 level teaspoon baking powder
110 g (4 oz) butter or margarine
225 g (8 oz) brown sugar (demerara)
2 large eggs (size 1)

To fill:
Apricot jam
Some of the chocolate icing

To decorate:
Chocolate icing (see next page).

Tin: Deep cake tin 20.5 cm-21.5 cm (8-8½") diameter lined with greaseproof paper, brushed with melted butter.

Cooking Time: 50-60 minutes (180°C, 350°F. Gas 4)

Put the cocoa into a bowl and mix it into a thick paste with the water. Then gradually stir in the yogurt to make a creamy chocolate mixture.

Sift the flour, bread soda and baking powder together into another container.

In a mixing bowl, beat the butter until soft. Then add in the sugar and beat. When they are nice and soft add one of the eggs along with two spoons of the sifted flour. Beat well. Add the second egg and a little more flour. Beat again. Next stir in the remaining flour along with the yogurt mixture. Stir gently but thoroughly together. Spoon into the prepared tin and spread out evenly.

Bake until cooked through. Test with a skewer which should come out clean with no dough-like particles attached. Stand the tin on a wire tray to cool. Cover with tin foil to keep in steam and so keep the top soft.

When cold, slit cake carefully to make two layers. Spread with apricot jam and some of the chocolate icing and sandwich together again.

Cover cake completely with most of the icing and put the remainder into an icing bag with a 'rose' nozzle and pipe 'roses' of icing around the top of the cake.

Allow to stand in a cool place for a few hours before serving. Cut in small slices.

Chocolate Icing

This icing is so nice you would eat it without the cake! The yogurt gives a lovely 'zap' to the flavour.

150 g (5 oz) good quality cooking chocolate (dark)
1 carton (125 ml) natural yogurt
200 ml (7 fl oz) fresh cream
50 g (2 oz) icing sugar, sifted

Melt the cooking chocolate, then stir in the yogurt to make a creamy mixture. Whisk the cream in a separate bowl until stiff and stir in the icing sugar, followed by the chocolate mixture. Cool in the fridge to thicken more. Then use as required.

Mincemeat and Almond Cake (F)

This recipe is ideal for "helter skelter" cooking - the last minute Christmas rush, or anytime you want to make a quick fruit cake, because it uses a jar of mincemeat. It can be eaten within a couple of days or kept for a few weeks.

450 g (1 lb) jar mincemeat
3-4 tablespoons Sherry OR Whiskey OR a liqueur
100 g (3½ oz) packet of flaked or chopped almonds
½-1 teaspoon almond essence
225 g (8 oz) margarine or butter (soft)
225 g (8 oz) brown sugar (demerara)
4 large eggs (size 1)
250 g (9 oz) flour (not self raising)
100 g (3½ oz) packet of ground almonds

Tin: Round cake tin 21.5 cm - 23 cm (8½"-9") in diameter. Line with greaseproof paper or baking parchment, brush with melted margarine.

Cooking Time: 2-3 hours (150°C, 300°F, Gas 2)

Empty the mincemeat into a bowl and add in the sherry, flaked almonds and essence. In a separate bowl beat the butter until soft. Then add in the brown sugar, the eggs and the flour. Mix together and then beat lightly to ensure an even mix.

Add in the mincemeat mixture and the ground almonds, stir through. Turn into the prepared tin and smooth the top.

Bake until cooked right through. Test centre with a skewer, if no doughlike particles adhere to it, the cake is cooked. If top is getting too brown during baking, cover tin with foil or reduce heat. Stand tin on a wire tray to cool.

Variation: Scatter 25 g (1 oz) flaked almonds over top of cake before baking.

Almond Feather Sponge (F)

Not only has this cake got a wonderful flavour, but it is so simple to make. Some ground almonds are included in the mixture and flaked almonds are scattered over the top.

175 g (6 oz) butter or margarine (soft)
175 g (6 oz) caster sugar
3 large eggs
Finely grated rind ½ lemon
½ level teaspoon almond essence
150 g (5 oz) self raising flour
75 g (3 oz) ground almonds

Topping:
25 g (1 oz) flaked almonds

Tin: A deepish sandwich tin, 21.5-23 cm diameter (8½"-9"). Grease well and dust with flour.

Cooking Time: Bake for about 35-45 minutes (180°C, 350°F, Gas 4).

All-in-one method: For this, be sure the butter or margarine is soft (I soften it in the microwave for about 20 seconds - but have to be careful not to melt it!).

To the softened butter/margarine, add all the other ingredients (except the flaked almonds). Mix very well together - but don't beat more than necessary. Turn into prepared tin. Smooth out and scatter the flaked almonds over the top.

Bake until a delightful golden brown and cooked through. Partly cool in tin then turn out and allow to cool completely. No icing is necessary.

Ginger and Banana Cake

The grated fresh root ginger is optional but has a delicious flavour. A great cake for lunch boxes.

225 g (8 oz) margarine or butter
2 bananas, peeled (225 g/8 oz)
1 carton (125 ml) yogurt (banana or hazelnut)
225 g (8 oz) caster sugar
2 eggs
175 g (6 oz) self raising flour
110 g (4 oz) wholemeal flour
1 teaspoon baking powder
2-4 heaped teaspoons freshly grated root ginger OR
1 heaped teaspoon ground ginger
50 g (2 oz) crystallized ginger, chopped (see note)
50 g (2 oz) chopped walnuts (optional)

Note: The crystallized ginger is also optional but has a lovely hot gingery flavour.

Tin: Loaf tin 23 cm x 12.5 cm x 7.5 cm deep (9" x 5" x 3" deep) greased and dusted with flour, line base with greaseproof paper.

Cooking Time: About 1¼-1½ hours (180°C, 350°F, Gas 4).

All-in-one method: For this, be sure the margarine/butter is soft. (I soften it in the microwave but take care not to melt it!).

Mash the bananas, to a purée and stir in the yogurt. Add to the softened margarine/butter, with all the other ingredients and mix very well. Don't beat more than necessary (as it toughens the flour).

Turn mixture into the prepared tin and bake until brown and cooked through. Check centre with a skewer. There should be no doughlike particles adhering to it. Cool cake in the tin standing on a wire tray. When cold turn out.

Ginger Glacé Icing (optional)

Pour **2-3 tablespoons boiling water** onto **2 teaspoons grated fresh root ginger.** Leave to stand for a couple of minutes. Strain off water and use just enough to moisten **175 g (6 oz) icing sugar** to make a fairly stiff icing. Spread over top of the cake.

My Mother's Almond Slices

I must have inherited my love of almonds from my mother. Tasty pastry spread with apricot jam, topped with almond meringue, scattered with chopped almonds. Cut in slices when baked.

Almond shortcrust pastry (see Strawberry Tart page 80)
Apricot jam
2 large egg whites
75 g (3 oz) caster sugar
50 g (2 oz) ground almonds
½ teaspoon almond essence (optional)
50 g (2 oz) chopped almonds

Tin: Rectangular tin, greased, 33 cm x 23 cm (13" x 9").

Cooking Time: For about 15 minutes (200°C, 400°F, Gas 6), then reduce heat (180°C, 350°F, Gas 4) and cook for about 10-20 minutes more.

Roll out the pastry and line the base (not the sides) of the tin. Spread a thin layer of apricot jam evenly all over the pastry.

Whisk the egg whites until just stiff. Whisk in the sugar a little at a time. Add in the ground almonds and the almond essence, whisk through. Don't mind if the egg whites lose some of their volume.

Spread the meringue over the jam, right out to the edge of the pastry. Scatter the chopped almonds on top and bake until golden brown and the pastry is cooked.

Cut into wide fingers or squares and cool on a wire tray.

Some products known as 'cooking chocolate' are, in fact, substitutes. A good **quality chocolate** can be determined by the amount of cocoa solids it contains. At least 30% is required - so read the small print!

Chocolate Clusters (Q)

(about 24)

Really simple to make. The mixture of juicy raisins and crunchy almonds in the chocolate is only gorgeous! These sweets make a lovely gift - so much more personal than a box of chocolates. Also they are ideal to serve with coffee after a special dinner.

110 g (4 oz) raisins
2-3 tablespoons liqueur OR Sweet Sherry
OR juice of an orange
50 g (2 oz) chopped almonds
175 g (6 oz) dark cooking chocolate
25 g (1 oz) butter
About 24 small, sweet sized paper cases (sometimes called
petit fours cases). (optional)

Put the raisins into a small saucepan with the liqueur (or sherry or orange juice). Cover with a lid and cook gently until the liquid is just absorbed by the fruit. Don't let it burn! Toast the chopped almonds until golden in a hot oven or under a grill for a few minutes. Don't let them burn!

Meanwhile, melt the chocolate and butter together. Then add in the raisins and nuts and stir well. Spoon into the small paper cases. If these are not available, spoon out mixture in little sweet-sized mounds onto baking parchment. Allow to cool and set.

If giving as a present put the sweets in a doily lined box.

Variation: Add **25 g (1 oz) finely chopped crystallized ginger** to the melted chocolate when mixing in the raisins and almonds. The ginger has a nice 'hot' flavour.

Macaroons (Q)

Crisp and chewey, I'd eat these 'til they came out my ears! They make a lovely gift at Christmas, or anytime. A mixture of egg whites, ground almonds and sugar is spooned onto rice paper and baked. Rice paper is edible and is available in newsagents and supermarkets.

100 g (3½ oz) packet of ground almonds
175 g (6 oz) caster sugar
25 g (1 oz) cornflour
25 g (1 oz) ground rice or semolina (optional)

3 egg whites
½ teaspoon almond essence
3-4 large sheets of rice paper
7-8 blanched almonds, split in half

Tin: 2-3 flat baking tins, lay rice paper on these.

Cooking Time: About 25 minutes (180°C, 350°F, Gas 4).

Mix the first four ingredients together in a bowl. The ground rice is optional - but if you have it, it gives a vague grittiness to the texture of the macaroons, which is rather nice.

In a separate bowl, whisk the egg whites and almond essence until they are frothy. Then stir this into the almond mixture, adding just enough to make a softish mixture, you may not need all the egg whites. If the mixture is too soft, the macaroons will just spread out too thinly. Put out in spoonfuls (2 rounded teaspoons each) onto the rice paper, leaving some space between for spreading out. Place a split almond on top of each one.

Bake in a moderate oven until they turn a nice pale golden colour. Tear away excess rice paper. Cool on a wire tray and then store in an air tight container - and hide them from me!

Popcorn Crispy Buns (Q)

Instead of Rice Krispies, freshly popped corn is mixed through melted chocolate. Popcorn contains natural fibre and has no added sugar. I enjoy these because they are not too sweet.

40 g (1½ oz) popping corn
A little oil
110 g (4 oz) cooking chocolate
Paper bun cases

To pop the corn: Put a very thin layer of oil in the bottom of a wide saucepan (preferably with a heavy base). Cover with a single layer of popping corn. Put the lid on and cook over gentle heat until you hear one pop! Draw off heat for 1 minute, then return and continue cooking over gentle heat, shaking all the time, until all the corn has popped.

Meanwhile melt the chocolate and add the popped corn and fill into the paper bun cases. Allow to cool and set.

Shortbread

One of life's little luxuries - especially when made with butter! The secret is to cook at low heat so that it only turns a pale golden colour.

110 g (4 oz) butter or margarine
50 g (2 oz) caster sugar
¼ teaspoon of vanilla essence
110 g (4 oz) flour
50 g (2 oz) ground rice OR semolina (optional, see note)

Note: The ground rice gives a nice subtle crunch to the shortbread, but if you prefer, substitute it with flour.

Tin: 20.5 cm-23 cm (8"-9") sandwich tin (or baking sheet), greased.

Cooking Time: About 45 minutes (150°C, 300°F, Gas 2).

Beat the butter until soft, then beat in the caster sugar and vanilla essence until soft and creamy. Mix together the flour and ground rice and add to the butter/sugar mixture, mixing to form a crumbly mixture. Use your hands to gather into a lump of dough.
Place dough in the tin and press out to evenly cover tin. Use a small glass jar (mustard!!) to roll and flatten the dough inside the tin. Then score a pattern with a fork around the edge (or pinch the dough at even intervals). Pierce holes with a fork into the shortbread here and there (to allow steam escape and prevent rising).

Bake in the oven until pale golden. If necessary lay a piece of greaseproof paper on top halfway through cooking to prevent colour getting too deep. When baked, cut with a sharp knife to mark out the slices but do not remove them from the tin until the shortbread has cooled. Stand tin on a wire tray while cooling.

Shortbread Biscuits

Make the shortbread dough as above and turn out onto floured surface. Roll out about 0.5 cm (¼ ") thick. Cut into circles with a biscuit/scone cutter (about 6-7.5 cm/2½"-3" in diameter). Place on greased baking trays with a little space between them. Bake as for shortbread - but they will cook more quickly (in about 20 minutes).

Fresh Ginger Shortbread (or Biscuits)

Use the same recipe as for Shortbread except include **1-2 heaped teaspoons of grated fresh root ginger,** (peel off woodlike skin), and **25 g (1 oz) of crystallized ginger,** finely chopped. Mix in before adding the flour. Make as for shortbread or shortbread biscuits. Before baking decorate each biscuit (or slice) with a **small thin slice of crystallized ginger.**

Orange and Raisin Muffins (Q) (F)

A quick muffin mix, using melted margarine. This amount makes 12 in a bun tray. The special muffin tins are twice the size of normal bun tins so this mixture will only make 6 of them. The tins need to be fairly full so when baked, the mixture rises right up.

225 g (8 oz) self raising flour
110 g (4 oz) caster sugar
Grated rind of 1 orange
50 g (2 oz) raisins
50 g (2 oz) chopped walnuts or almonds
110 g (4 oz) margarine
1 large egg
110 ml (4 fl oz) fresh milk
Juice of 1 orange
½ teaspoon vanilla essence

Tin: Bun tray or muffin tray lined with paper bun cases.

Cooking Time: 20-30 minutes (200°C, 400°F, Gas 6).

Put the first five ingredients into a bowl and mix together.

Melt the margarine, cool it somewhat, add in the remaining ingredients and mix well. Add the liquid to the dry ingredients and mix to a fairly wet mixture. Spoon into the paper cases filling them right up.

Bake until golden and cooked through. Serve warm or cold.

Chocolate Muffins (Q) (F)

Make the same recipe as for the Orange and Raisin Muffins except add **15 g (½ oz) cocoa** to the flour mixture. Use only **25 g (1 oz) raisins** and add **50 g (2 oz) of dark cooking chocolate,** chopped up. Also add just a **hint extra of milk** (because of the cocoa).

Wedding Cake

Rich fruit cakes store well because of the sugar in the fruit. The longer they are stored the darker they get. Butter keeps cakes fresh longer. My personal preference is for a 'young' cake - 3-6 weeks old!

Three Tier Wedding Cake

If round tins are preferred - use a tin 2.5 cm (1") larger than stated for square tins.

INGREDIENTS FOR 28 CM (11") SQUARE TIN

2 packets (375 g/13 oz each) raisins
2 packets (375 g/13 oz each) sultanas
3 cartons (100 g/3½ oz each) glacé cherries
2 cartons (100 g/3½ oz each) mixed peel
110 g (4 oz) figs
50 g (2 oz) crystallized ginger
2 tablespoons tinned strawberries (juice drained off)
Grated rind of 1 orange and 1 lemon
4 tablespoons whiskey
1 packet (100 g/3½ oz) ground almonds
1 packet (100 g/3½ oz) chopped almonds
500 g (18 oz) flour (not self-raising)
1 rounded teaspoon each nutmeg, cinnamon and ground cloves
450 g (1 lb) butter or margarine
450 g (1 lb) brown sugar (demerara)
8 large eggs (at room temperature)

INGREDIENTS FOR 23 CM (9") SQUARE TIN

1½ packets (560 g/20 oz) raisins
1 packet (375 g/13 oz) sultanas
2 cartons (100 g/3½ oz each) glacé cherries
2 cartons (100 g/3½ oz each) mixed peel
75 g (3 oz) figs
40 g (1½ oz) crystallized ginger
2 tablespoons tinned strawberries (juice drained off)

Grated rind of a ½ lemon and ½ orange
2 tablespoons whiskey
1 packet (100 g/3½ oz) chopped almonds
50 g (2 oz) ground almonds
400 g (14 oz) flour (not self-raising)
1 level teaspoon each nutmeg, cinnamon and ground cloves
350 g (12 oz) butter or margarine
350 g (12 oz) brown sugar (demerara)
6 large eggs (at room temperature)

INGREDIENTS FOR 15 CM (6") SQUARE TIN

175 g (6 oz) raisins
175 g (6 oz) sultanas
1 carton (100 g/3½ oz) glacé cherries
1 carton (100 g/3½ oz) mixed peel
25 g (1 oz) figs
15 g (½ oz) crystallized ginger
1 tablespoon tinned strawberries, juice drained off
Grated rind of ¼ lemon and ¼ orange
1 tablespoon whiskey
50 g (2 oz) chopped almonds
50 g (2 oz) ground almonds
150 g (5 oz) flour (not self-raising)
¼ teaspoon each nutmeg, cinnamon and ground cloves
110 g (4 oz) butter or margarine
110 g (4 oz) brown sugar (demerara)
2 large eggs (at room temperature)

Prepare tins (all sizes)
Since rich fruit cakes require long, slow cooking, it is important to line tins well. Line the outside of the tins with a layer of strong brown paper tied on with string. Then line the insides with a double layer of greaseproof paper. Pay careful attention to neat square corners. Finally, brush the greaseproof lining with melted butter.

Prepare fruit (all sizes)
Remove any stalks from raisins and sultanas. Chop cherries, figs and crystallized ginger. Mix all the fruit in a bowl with the drained strawberries, the orange and lemon rinds. Add the whiskey. Leave to steep overnight to allow the fruit to soak up the juices. Just before using, stir in the ground and chopped almonds.

Prepare the cake mixture

Be careful not to overbeat the cake mixture as this entraps too much air, which when baked in the oven results in a loose, open textured cake. This can be a cause of fruit falling.

Mix the spices with the flour, leave to one side. Beat the butter until soft, then add in the sugar and beat until mixture is soft. Beat in the eggs one at a time adding a little of the weighed flour with each one. When all the eggs are added, stir in the remaining flour. Stir the fruit mixture through the cake mixture gently, but thoroughly. Spoon into the tin and spread evenly out. Cover the top of the tin with a layer of foil that folds down over the side linings of the tin.

Oven temperature and times

Long slow cooking is important for a rich fruit cake. (Cook cakes separately.) Sit cake (all sizes) below the centre of oven, preheated, (140°C, 275°F, Gas 1) and cook for the following times, approximately.

15 cm (6") cake takes about 2½-3½ hours
23 cm (9") cake takes about 3½-4¾ hours
28 cm (11") cake takes about 5-6 hours

Remember, ovens vary, so it is necessary to use your own judgement. The 23 cm (9") and 28 cm (11") cake will begin to look 'set', not browned, after about 1½-2½ hours. Avoid opening the oven door more than necessary (and do it gently).

To test if cooked, pierce with a skewer, which must come out with no dough-like particles adhering to it. Cook for longer if necessary.

To store

Cool the cake in the tin standing on a wire tray. Sprinkle the cake with more whiskey while it is still hot. When it is cold, wrap it in greaseproof paper, then in foil and place in a plastic bag and store in a cool, airy place. The occasional little dash of whiskey or brandy over the top during storing is good for the flavour.

INDEX

Index of Anything I Can Do... Cookbook

I include this index for the greater convenience of the owners of my two cookery books